When the Heart Speaks, Listen

Discovering Inner Wisdom

Lerita Coleman Brown, Ph.D.

Second printing

Some names and identifying details may have been changed to protect the privacy of individuals.

ISBN: 978-0-578-73011-0
www.peaceforhearts.com

When the Heart Speaks, Listen is printed in Garamond

This book is dedicated to:

My heart donor, Jody; her brother, Cameron; and the entire Goetz family for their decision to give the gift of life;

Jennifer Lund, my kidney donor, affectionately known as my kidney sister; and

All individuals and donor families who have chosen to give the gift of life.

Acknowledgments

I am indebted to so many people who have been a part of my transplant journey, and who have helped through the various stages of preparing my heart dialogues for publication.

I would like to begin by thanking my immediate family—Mom, Dad, Leroy, Clarence and Lisa—and my extended family in Colorado, including the Boulder Mothers (Mildred Nilon, Ellen Tate, and Martie Bauduit), Thelma Craig, Terry Cohen, Gary McClelland, Mary Ann Shea, Letitia Williams, Mette Riis, Ron Bonial, Peter Groff, as well as friends and family of my donor, Jody Goetz—Cameron Goetz, Lillian Miller, and Cathy Brase. I am most grateful for my support sisters—Shirley Stancato, Beverly Coleman-Anderson, Roberta Sanders, Marie Kemp, Betty Gillespie, Bobbi Fueri and Linda Hornbeak-Ferguson, each of whom took a week to care for me after Mom's family leave ended. I cannot imagine having better medical and psychological support from the then University of Colorado Health Science Center in Denver, with special affection for my primary transplant physician, JoAnn Lindenfeld, M.D., and my trusted and brilliant psychotherapist in Boulder, Ricardo Esparza, Ph.D., who wisely advised me to talk with my heart.

A special thanks goes to Joan Bolker, my writing coach at the Writing Center at Harvard University, who taught me to love writing, and Barbara Rosenberg, who offered comments on an earlier draft. Others who cheered my writings of these conversations and read excerpts include James Henderson, Teri Hernandez, Beth Darnall, Leah Pressman, Ruth Wilson, Harry Jackson, Jr., Ann Hopkins, Art Jones, Paule'-Elizabeth Jackson, Renee Moody, Susan Hodges, Linda Jackson, Tanzania Nevels, Jennifer Lund, Beth Hackett, Emily Gwynn, Jan Willis, Betsy Balford, Carl McColman, Veronica Henson-Phillips, Shirlene Holmes, Karen Henderson, Valinda Brown, and Peggy Thompson.

Thank you also to the members of my "Artist Way" group—Jocelyn Lyons, Marquita Jackson-Bradley, and Shay Dowley; Spirit Sisters Betty Cunningham, Linda Bryant, Joan Murray, and Florida Ellis; and my monthly Sistas in Silence group members, who continue to sustain me—some of whom both read my dialogues and supported me with many forms of spiritual and emotional care.

Without the keen and spiritual eyes of my marvelous copy editor, Sabbaye McGriff, my words would lack some of their sparkle. I am so grateful to Shirley Paulk for introducing us. I have no words to express my gratitude for my loving and caring husband, Columbus Brown, who leaped onto the roller coaster ride that is the life we've led together for nearly 20 years. I thank you for being present for all of the hospital/clinic visits, for praying me alive when I thought my life was over, for creating space and time for many silent retreats, and for possessing lots of patience and a listening heart.

Most of all, I thank Sophia, my nickname for Spirit, which lies within my heart and continues to give me strength, unfathomable wisdom, and daily guidance to face whatever comes my way.

Contents

About the Author

Lerita Coleman Brown, Ph.D. and Ayśe I. Carden Distinguished Professor Emerita of Psychology at Agnes Scott College, has survived 25 years with a transplanted heart, 15 of them with a transplanted kidney as well. Since her transplants, she also endured a heart valve replacement and a pacemaker implant. Her medical ordeals fostered an unwavering advocacy of organ and tissue donation, contemplative spirituality, explorations of inner life, and the wisdom of Howard Thurman, all of which she promotes at peaceforhearts.com, and on social media.

When the Heart Speaks, Listen

Discovering Inner Wisdom

PART 1
Introduction

Hearts are full of wisdom. How do I know? I discovered the profound insights of the heart I was born with when I lost it and received a new one during a heart transplant. To prepare for this "change in heart," I began conversing with my old and new hearts.

Early on, my hearts made it clear that they wanted to communicate with me. Initially, I ignored their sage counsel, offered through whispers and quiet urgings. Instead, I thought *I* knew best. As our conversations grew deeper, I learned how misguided I was.

When people speak of the heart, their comments and observations depend on their perspective. Doctors—cardiologists more specifically—view with intrigue this wondrous muscle responsible for pumping blood to our vital organs. Some people immediately think about emotions and focus on whether they or others feel happy, sad or angry. The more philosophical among us ponder what the heart symbolizes as the core of our being. Often people associate the heart with notions of romance and falling in love. Still, others link the heart to pursuing one's passions as in "following your heart." It is rarer, however, especially in today's world, for people to think of the heart as the source of spiritual guidance or the seat of sacred wisdom.

Talking with my hearts introduced me to another world as I learned how my hearts think or feel about what I say or do. Through these dialogues, I also learned that hearts possess physical, dispositional, emotional, and spiritual characteristics. The greatest lesson they taught me was that inner listening is key; that accessing the wisdom of the heart remains unattainable unless one is willing to pause, listen, and pay attention to it.

Our conversations began when I noticed my life unraveling. I needed some method to cope with the hysteria and anxiety I felt over needing a heart transplant at age 41. As a single, childless, African American, professional woman without a significant relationship at the time, I knew of no other way to survive but to pray and plead with my heart for some direction.

Fortunately, Carlos Martinez, my very wise and supportive psychotherapist, suggested I talk with my heart. At first, I thought his proposal was psychobabble, another silly New Age technique to waste my precious time. Little did I know that it was a common Jungian practice called "active imagination" that many therapists employ to help clients uncover and utilize their inner wisdom. Could my heart guide me now?

My history of heart problems was long but not particularly dramatic, nothing in the league of a heart transplant. I could hardly utter the words, let alone contemplate what they might mean to me and my life. The idea felt like I was being kidnapped and thrown into the middle of a science fiction, horror movie.

Relinquishing my heart provided a special trauma for me. When I was nine months old, I was diagnosed with a heart murmur of some unknown and mysterious origin. It was not until nearly 20 years later that the medical community labeled this heart disease "idiopathic hyper-tropic sub-aortic stenosis (IHSS)," now known as HCM or hyper-tropic cardiomyopathy, and a set of symptoms that identified the genetic disorder underlying it. At first, I did not consider having this "heart condition" throughout childhood and early adolescence a serious problem until I encountered all the restrictions that accompanied it—no volleyball team, no cheerleader tryouts, and perhaps no children. My pediatric cardiologist suggested that I could possibly pursue a muted career such as a librarian, lest I die of overstimulation or strain.

My heart became the decision maker of my life. Was it too cold for me to walk to the library? Could I dance for an entire song? What about travel abroad? Would graduate school be too stressful? Now the center of my daily life, how could I bear to let my heart go? Yet I was trapped. The doctors made it very clear: Without a heart transplant I faced certain death in 18 months or less.

My medical team, well versed in performing transplants, had no idea how to calculate or treat the psychic toll the loss of one's heart can exact. I expended an enormous amount of energy agonizing over the decision as fear of the unknown immobilized me. Once I began the journey, my odyssey through a heart transplant was at times physically and emotionally gut-wrenching as changes in medications, threats of rejection and infections permeated my life. But this book is not just about experiencing a heart transplant. It also is about opening up my heart, examining its contents, and allowing it to become my guide. The dialogues I share illustrate how my heart, despite its inevitable demise, ushers me through the process of letting it go and prepares me for life with a new one.

Part One begins with the moment I learned my heart condition had deteriorated to the point that I needed a heart transplant. It chronicles how, in my panic, desperation and fear, I begin to commune with my ailing heart. It is through a series of these dialogues that I learn about the physical, spiritual and emotional aspects of the heart.

Part Two involves conversations with my new heart. These dialogues are often strained and awkward because my new heart is a stranger and I am a foreigner to it. Spanning 21 months, these chats illustrate our struggle to adapt to a new life together. My new heart slowly leads me into a deeper exploration of the spiritual guidance that hearts offer and how regular inner listening facilitates a life of greater peace and joy.

To manage the volatile mix of physical, psychological, emotional, and spiritual challenges a heart transplant presents, my hearts—old and new—help me to uncover the wealth of wisdom that hearts hold. Now I wish to share the insights and the process with others. My hearts, for example, teach me that no matter what I *say* or *do*, it is what I *feel* in my heart that matters most. They share other basic universal truths like *"True happiness is not about having things but about having a happy heart."* They remind me that it is my heart's desire to sing and dance, and when it does, I feel joy. Yet my heart cannot sing or dance if the heart space is clogged up with emotional baggage, including old wounds and resentments.

Furthermore, unhealthy eating habits and lack of exercise increase its load. I cannot fully utilize the heart's deeper wisdom unless I release the issues that weigh it down. These and other revelations accompany me on my journey to switch hearts. Despite my initial reluctance and resistance to the idea of a transplant, I now realize what wonderful spiritual awakening this modern-day medical miracle and trauma brought me.

Have you felt your heart attempt to communicate with you? Have you ever tried to talk with your heart? How would you describe your heart? Does it possess a particular character? Is it anxious, angry, peaceful, or hopeful? And how might it describe you? These are among the questions suggested for reflection after each conversation. Writing your own heart conversations and answering some of the reflection questions may evoke unpleasant emotions, which can be productive areas for further reflection. You may want to consider exploring these feelings more deeply with a spiritual director/companion, psychotherapist, pastoral counselor or other health professional. I hope, though, in pondering my heart dialogues, you will be inspired to listen to and talk with your own heart. If you do, I am certain that it will lead you to uncover the peace, joy and inner wisdom your heart holds for you.

Lerita Coleman Brown

Prologue

"What a beautiful pristine Colorado winter morning," I thought. The sun slowly brightened the azure blue sky with a tinge of yellow-orange and the frosty crisp air bit my face as I opened the garage door. Living at a high altitude, the sunlight shone so brightly, I found sunglasses to be a necessity, not an option. Everything—trees, grass, even the asphalt—vibrated with life the day after a snowstorm. Driving toward the interstate, I could hear my tires rolling through the wet and slightly slushy streets. I was on my way to a rare early morning appointment with my gynecologist. Lord knows, I didn't want to start the day with a doctor's visit like that, but the next available appointment was months off. One of the few doctors I actually liked and admired, Dr. Robert Barnes, an African-American physician in his mid-forties, had a very popular practice with African-American, White, Hispanic and Asian patients, as well as a multi-cultural office staff.

Approaching Interstate 25 from Highway 36, otherwise known as the Boulder-Denver Turnpike, I wondered if I might encounter rush hour traffic. I checked the time on the dashboard of my dark blue Honda Prelude, and it appeared that I would arrive at Dr. Barnes' office with a few minutes to spare. It brought to mind that song we sang in elementary school: "Oh what a beautiful morning, oh what a beautiful day, I've got a wonderful feeling, everything's going my way."

Suddenly, it felt as if some force jumped into the driver's seat and took over the controls. The car veered sharply to the right while I desperately tried to hold the steering wheel steady and turn it to the left, but to no avail. I had hit a patch of black ice, and the car was sliding and twirling across three lanes of traffic! My life flashed before my eyes at the thought that at any minute, some car racing on the right side would slam into me. Holding on for dear life, I screamed, "Sweet Jesus," as the car spun around in circles until it came to a stop on the shoulder, nearly in a ditch and turned in the opposite direction to ongoing traffic. I sat there for a moment shaking and praying, grateful that I had not become an accident victim. I looked around as traffic continued moving past me on the highway. I turned off the engine and checked my watch. I knew I would be late, since there was no way I could drive with a shaking body and chattering teeth. Each time I placed my foot near the pedal, it quivered so much I couldn't hold it in place. I took some deep breaths anticipating my next challenge—how to enter the highway from the wrong way.

After a few minutes of deep breathing, I sensed it was time to approach the highway. I started my engine, shifted into drive and put on my turn signal. Fortunately, some kind man saw my dilemma and slowed, holding up a line of traffic to allow me to enter and turn my car around, so it headed in the right direction in the far right lane. Still slightly trembling, I slowly steered a few exits down to reach the professional office building near downtown Denver.

Later, when Dr. Barnes entered the exam room, he looked at me and said, "You look like a ghost. What happened to you?" I told him about the near accident as he listened to my heart and took my pulse.

"How have you been feeling in general?" he asked.

"You know, about the same," I replied. "I have noticed, though, that when I walk around the golf course near my house in the mornings, I seem to have to stop and rest. I don't understand it. It's not like the path sits on a hill or anything."

"Maybe you need to check in with your cardiologist while you are in Denver today. Isn't he at St. Joseph?" he asked as he performed my pelvic exam.

"Yeah, but I don't know if I can walk in," I murmured.

"I'll have my nurse call. You get dressed, and we'll talk in the office," he said.

Still reverberating from the morning, I took off the hospital gown and got dressed. I slowly walked down the hall to his office, where I sat looking at the lovely pen set and ink blotter on the gorgeous mahogany desk, the diplomas hanging on the wall and the plush chairs. Dr. Barnes' practice was flourishing. I felt proud to see a black doctor, a black man doing so well. In the '90s, there were approximately 100,000 black people living in the Denver Metro area, who were largely responsible for electing a black mayor, but that certainly did not fit the stereotype of Colorado.

Dr. Barnes walked into the office and informed me that my cardiologist office had confirmed that they could fit me in early that afternoon around 1 p.m. "There are some great places for lunch near his office. After that, you need to go home and get some rest," he advised. "You've had quite a day, and we don't want anything to happen to you. I mean, how many Black professors do we have at CU these days?"

"Not many," I said, laughing. "All right, I'll go see my cardiologist. Actually, I could use a nice leisurely lunch for a change. Eating a nice salad with a piece of French bread would calm my nerves. That near crash spooked me this morning."

"Really, Lerita, you must take care of yourself. Don't let those folks at the university drive you nuts," Dr. Barnes instructed.

"I promise I won't. I'll see you in about six months, okay?"

"Okay." He smiled and shook my hand as I left the office.

I took my time getting back to the car. I was grateful for Dr. Barnes' affirming and reassuring demeanor. For me, it made such a difference when I could connect with my doctor.

I started the car, and my thoughts immediately flowed back to the morning's events. It's funny how terror operates. It is not easy to shake off. No matter what I did, change radio stations, repeat a mantra, I still felt frazzled from the morning brush with catastrophe.

I arrived about 15 minutes early for my appointment at St. Joseph Hospital's cardiology practice, where the receptionist informed me that Dr. Desai Patel could see me today but wanted me to have an echocardiogram first. I trudged down the hallway recalling the many times I had performed this routine. With a heart problem like IHSS, I think I started having echocardiograms in 1975. Sound waves appeared to be the best way to track my heart problem. At least it wasn't as bad as having the dreaded heart catheterization, a more invasive procedure with catheters going up the artery in the groin.

I opened the door to the exam room, which had a special padded table with a cutout platform that lowered right in front near the heart. A large echocardiogram machine sat next to the table with lots of dials, a screen, probes and gel. It also contained a slot for videotapes, which they used to track my "echoes," from one visit to the next. Lying on the exam table was the unisex, one-size-fits-all gown that nearly swallows me and which I never know from one visit to the next if it ties to the front or back. Either way, I always feel too cold with one half of my body exposed.

Leslie, one of my favorite echo techs, walked into the room. "Hey, Lerita, how are you?" she asked.

"Well, outside of a near-death experience this morning, things are okay. I noticed though, that I've been getting a little tired on my morning walk, and as usual, I have a ton of work at the office. Overall, I'm pretty good."

"Okay, let's get started. I see you have the gown tied to the front. Why don't you lie down on your side facing me? Now I hope you're ready, because you know this gook is pretty cold."

She moved the probe with the cold gel around my chest, holding it in some places longer than others. There was my pumping heart on the black and white screen—as fuzzy looking as those sonograms of fetuses. As I lay there looking at the ceiling, I wondered why everything revolves around my heart. I almost had a major automobile accident today, and we are looking at my heart. This is so crazy.

As Leslie was about to finish up, Dr. Patel walked into the room.

"Ah, Ms. Coleman, how are you? Let's take a look at this echo. Okay..." as he stood staring at the screen. "It looks as if your IHSS has evolved into full-blown cardiomyopathy. Uh, you may be looking at a heart transplant in about three to four years." Then Dr. Patel turned and walked out of the door.

I turned to Leslie. "WHAT?" "Did I hear him right? Did he say something about a heart transplant?" I blurted out, almost falling off of the exam table, gook sliding down toward my stomach.

"It appears so," Leslie replied.

She looked as incredulous as I did. How could a doctor convey news like that and walk out of the room? It all seemed so surreal, and suddenly I felt like I was caught in a real daytime nightmare. How could this be? I had open-heart surgery 15 years ago, and I thought I was finished. I tried to remain calm and not create a scene in the doctor's office, but the inner trembling returned. I wanted to scream and burst out crying, "*What do you mean a heart transplant—I thought I was done?!! Wasn't open-heart surgery in the middle of graduate school enough? Oh God, are you serious?*"

"I'll let you get dressed, Lerita," Leslie offered. "I will walk out with you."

I quickly threw on my clothes, realizing that this was the second time today I'd performed this task. However, this time I didn't care about how I looked. All I wanted was to get home. Leslie accompanied me to my car. "Do you think you will be all right driving back to Boulder?" she inquired. I was happy that someone was paying attention to my plight. I felt damn near hysterical at this point, but I held it in.

"Yeah, I'll be fine, Leslie. I'm going to pick up some food for dinner and head home for a long nap. Thanks so much for caring and walking me to my car."

As I drove home, tears rolled down my face and onto my sweater. How could this be happening? The day began perfectly, and after a frightening near-catastrophic car accident, the real crash was the shocking news that I would need a heart transplant! What kind of day, no, what kind of life was this? Reality, as I knew it, was about to be turned upside down, and my life would never be the same.

Talking to My Heart?

My first visit to the Heart Failure/Transplant Clinic at the University of Colorado Health Science Center in Denver is complete. It's September, 1994, and my "heart condition," IHSS, is officially a life-threatening heart muscle disease or cardiomyopathy. I am in need of a heart transplant very soon. Dr. Sarah Bloomberg suggests I schedule a transplant workup. I'm not ready to give up my precious heart although it clearly is failing more each day.

Back home, I eye the oxygen tank in the corner of my bedroom and the basket of pills sitting next to the television. My bloated stomach and ankles, that look like sausages remind me of the three months prior to my first open heart surgery in 1979. Then, I could barely walk across Harvard Yard to Widener Library from my office in William James Hall. I noticed the shortness of breath, the huffing and puffing as I trek to my office from my car. I feel exhausted all of the time. I cannot deny the fact that my body is rapidly deteriorating. Alone in my home, I cannot believe I am about to have open-heart surgery again, and a heart transplant no less!

I had been in and out of therapy for a number of years, as personal crises, like losing a job, a few unsuccessful romantic relationships and now an impending heart transplant punctuated my life. On my next visit to my trusted psychotherapist, Dr. Martinez, I presented my dilemma: How can I give up my beloved heart? I am anxious to hear his expert opinion because he specializes in working with people with chronic illnesses.

Besides feeling like an 8.0 earthquake blew up my life, with walls and windows crumbling all around me, there is so much to sort through. Do I really want to have a heart transplant? Am I ready to die if I choose not to have one? I yearn to have conversations about the entire transplant journey with family and friends, yet their refrain, "Consider the alternative," has become a mantra. I actually want to ponder the alternative—what it might mean to die—but people refuse to entertain the thought, let alone talk with me about it.

However, the message from the transplant team is as clear as a mountain river stream; the maximum time I have with this heart is approximately 18 months. Here I am at that fork in the road where one arrow points to an unfamiliar life as an organ transplant recipient and the other arrow points directly to death—another unknown territory but with much darker overtones.

What am I going to do with someone else's heart? I can't bear the thought of living without my heart. How can I make such a decision? Dr. Martinez asks me what my heart thinks about all of this. He suggests that I talk with my heart—that we should make the decision together.

Is he crazy? What does he mean, "Talk with my heart?" Have I ever communicated with my heart? Has *it* ever tried to talk with me? How am I going to talk to my heart?

Dr. Martinez recommends that I sit down with a yellow pad or at my computer and engage in a practice called "active imagination." I'm not certain how talking with my heart will help, but I am willing to try.

The next morning, I sit down with my pen and yellow pad and start writing. The following is my first attempt to contact my heart.

LERITA: OK, my dear heart. I think it's time for us to talk.

HEART: (no answer).

LERITA: Heart, I know you are there. I can feel you beating.

HEART: (no answer).

LERITA: Crap, would you answer?

HEART: (no answer)

LERITA: The medical folks are ready to take you out.

HEART: I know. I know. I'm not doing very well. I'm having a tough time.

LERITA: You *are* there. Gosh, I didn't think you would ever answer.

HEART: Like I said, I am having a hard time.

LERITA: You don't have to convince me. Is there anything I can do?

HEART: Fine time for you to be asking that question. You wait until I'm failing!? When it's almost impossible for me to pump basic fluids through your body and you ask, "Is there anything I can do?"

LERITA: You sound angry.

HEART: Yes, I am angry and very tired.

LERITA: Well you have some nerve. I need a heart transplant! I haven't had a date in three years or a decent boyfriend in about 15. Basically, all I do is work, pay my bills and feel exhausted. I can barely cook my meals let alone have any kind of social life because I am tired all of the time. The doctors tell me I need a new heart. You're not the only one angry. I am angry with you for falling down on the job!

HEART: Me? Falling down on the job? Do you know how many hours per week I put in? Do you realize I pump while you are asleep? Would you like for me to calculate it out for you? Let's see 7 X 24=168 hours per week. Do you put in anything close to that in your workweek? And let's not talk about the overtime!

LERITA: (Screaming) OVERTIME?! THERE ARE NO MORE THAN 168 HOURS IN A WEEK! HOW COULD THERE BE OVERTIME?!

HEART: Lerita, you are yelling, and that won't help either one of us. Could you lower your voice?

LERITA: You've got a lot of nerve asking me to lower my voice. OK. All right. What's this about overtime? And how do you know my name?

HEART: That's a silly question. I am your heart, and I live inside of you. How could I not know your name? But speaking of overtime…

LERITA: Yeah, let's talk about the overtime stuff. What are you calling overtime?

HEART: Let's try stress and being on the go all of the time. Have you ever thought that you try to fit too many things in one day? Do you know how to relax and *do nothing*? Do you know how to just *be* as in human *be-ing*?

LERITA: It seems like I've heard this before.

HEART: Yeah. Yeah. Yeah. You need the threat of a damn heart transplant to get your attention, huh? I've been trying to get through to you for years, especially since you jumped on that bandwagon in high school.

LERITA: What bandwagon?

HEART: The "I've got to be Miss It… somebody famous… Miss Perfectionist…prove to everyone that I'm at the top" bandwagon.

LERITA: Am I *that* bad?

HEART: Yes. Even now, you still over prepare for classes and presentations. You go over material that you already know backwards and forwards. Thank

God we've passed the days when you roll out of bed and perch in front of that computer all day and night.

LERITA: OK, so I am a workaholic.

HEART: Ha! That's putting it mildly. Has there ever been a day when you didn't have a list?

LERITA: I don't carry a list *every* day.

HEART: Would you like me to count the days on *one* hand that you *haven't* made a list? You even have one on the weekends.

LERITA: OK. You're right. I do push it a little bit.

HEART: A little bit? The key word here is PUSH. Do you understand how I might get tired because you are so driven? What is the goal? What are you striving for?

LERITA: You know, I really don't know. I figure I need to do something extraordinary.

HEART: See I told you. You are still on that bandwagon. You don't count graduating from high school in the top ten percent of your class and college with highest honors *extraordinary*? You don't consider getting a Ph.D. from Harvard *extraordinary*? And oh, by the way, having open-heart surgery in the middle of graduate school, that wasn't *extraordinary*? You don't believe being a professor at the University of Michigan *extraordinary* or working with your colleagues at Tennessee *extraordinary*? Being the only African-American professor in the psychology department at the University of Colorado isn't *extraordinary*? How about publishing over 30 book chapters and journal articles in addition to editing a book? That wasn't *extraordinary*? And making most of the beautiful clothes in your closet isn't *extraordinary*? How about not having missed more than a couple of days of work in over 15 years? If you don't think that you are *extraordinary*, your mind is sicker than I thought, and if that is the case, we're both in big trouble.

LERITA: How so?

HEART: I cannot take it. I can't push anymore. I'm tired. It's time for a rest. If you were to die tomorrow, and I'm sorry, I know it's a sensitive subject right now, but I think many people would agree that you've led an extraordinary life. Not merely by your accomplishments, though they are definitely impressive, but by your *presence*—the way you are with people, the wisdom you share. Look at

21

how students flock to your classes. What more goals and aspirations could you have?

LERITA: Oh, I don't know. I've given up wanting to win the Nobel Prize. I don't think I am going to have children and I'm almost fine with that. I figured since I didn't succeed at being a professor I could become a great writer.

HEART: Boy you are a hard driver. What more do you have to do to be a successful professor?

LERITA: I feel like I let down my colleagues.

HEART: Let's be real specific. It's Heathcliff.

LERITA: Well yes. He recruited me here to Colorado, and he had a different vision for me and higher expectations I suppose. He saw me as a potential star.

HEART: Are you on the earth to please Heathcliff or to please yourself? And what about pleasing God?

LERITA: God? You mean in my career? Pleasing myself? Well, that sounds so selfish.

HEART: Now we're getting somewhere. Do you think you would like to be Heathcliff? Is he a role model for you?

LERITA: Not really. I like his ability to concentrate and to get things done. He publishes a lot. I'm not sure if he likes to teach. I feel like he needs to be perfect. On the other hand, he does have a heart of gold. He helped me a lot throughout my career. I feel like I have disappointed him and a lot of other people too.

HEART: Heart of gold? Hmm. Why are you trying to please him? He doesn't pay your bills, and he's not living *your* life. When it is all said and done—I'm sorry to bring up death again, but I think it is relevant here—what are you going to do when you get to the gates of heaven when they ask you about your life? Are you going to say I spent it trying to be like Heathcliff? I cannot believe you would spend your life worshipping him. Besides, do you realize that no matter what you do, you will never get his approval?

LERITA: I don't worship him. I hate to disappoint people. You mean he will never think I am a star?

HEART: You know he is driven too. You two are just alike. You both spend enormous amounts of energy trying to be stars and wanting to be perfect.

LERITA: Yeah I'm familiar with the routine.

22

HEART: Think of the real stars that populate the heavens, Lerita. They don't have to do anything to shine. It's similar to the lovely flowers in your garden. They don't *try* to be beautiful, they just are. That's because they are fulfilling their purpose. And anything or anybody who is fulfilling his or her purpose in this world naturally shines and spreads joy.

LERITA: Hmm, that sounds very astute. I shouldn't try to be a star?

HEART: Lerita, we all know a star when we see one—human or otherwise. They shine because they are not letting anything block the Divine Light that shines through them.

LERITA: Whoa. I need to think about that. You're saying that I need to be myself and I need to please God. How do I do that?

HEART: Well you've gotten off to a good start. That exercise you did last week about opening up your heart and looking inside was excellent. Look at what you found in there. Lerita, you have such unrealistic expectations about everything. I mean do you need to win some award like the Nobel Prize to feel good about yourself? Why put all of that pressure on yourself?

LERITA: Yeah, that "opening up my heart" exercise was revealing. There was a ton of stuff in there. It's so hard to let go of wanting to be a star.

HEART: I understand that you grew up in a culture like Southern California where stardom is glorified. I am certain Mom and Dad, like most parents, wanted you to achieve some fame. But what do you think you are modeling to yourself and others when you engage in such madness? Don't you see how you are contributing to your own unhappiness and the insanity of everyone around you by participating in such a sham?

LERITA: I understand, I think. It's tough to change.

HEART: Knowing you, I doubt that you realize that having a heart transplant is the next extraordinary thing you will add to your list. Which reminds me (sighing), is there anything else?

LERITA: Besides becoming a famous writer?

HEART: Help me, Lord. My days are numbered. Come on, Lerita. Do you want to keep me or not?

LERITA: Now that is a good question. I am angry with you for giving me so much trouble over the years. It's terrifying to think that you might stop pumping. I was especially afraid when I was a little girl.

HEART: I'm sorry about that, Lerita. Maybe we can talk more about your difficulties with me when you were a child. But remember you didn't begin to experience serious problems until your junior year in college. That's when you became extremely ambitious and when the docs started you on medication to relax me. Think about it. You take medication to relax my muscles while you run around like a crazy woman. Does that make any sense? How about a pill to get that mind of yours to slow down? Lord knows you never stop thinking and you never stop worrying about things. If I scared you, I'm sorry, but I could sure use some help from you.

LERITA: I cannot believe I am having a conversation with my failing heart about being driven. What else can I do? You know this heart disease has thrown me behind schedule.

HEART: I think we need a more permanent solution. Even if you get a new heart, you will wear it out too if you keep up this pace. Clearly, we need to have some more discussions, because it is apparent that either you've been misinformed, misguided or you lack basic information about how hearts in truth operate. On the practical side, why don't you try to lighten up a bit so we might be able stay together longer. The longer we stay together the more knowledge I can share with you.

LERITA: (Sighing) Alright.

HEART: At least you will be in better shape for the next heart. Let's talk again next week. OK?

LERITA: OK.

Reflections

In what ways are you extraordinary? Ordinary?

Can you think of ways you may be putting undue stress on your heart in pursuit of your goals?

What might you ask your heart if you chose to have a conversation with it?

Have You Noticed Your Life Lately?

The cold crispness of an early fall Colorado morning slaps my face as soon as I open the door. It is 6:30 a.m. A dear friend, Rebecca Riddell, and I are both dressed in navy blue jumpers and white blouses. We decided to dress up for our foray to University Hospital for the transplant work-up. We laugh because we certainly make a noticeable pair. Rebecca is tall, white and pale with long auburn hair. She fits my stereotype of a model more than a physics professor. I, on the other hand, am a short, petite, brown skin woman with jet-black hair and equally dark eyes. Most people never guess that I am a professor either. Luckily, I avoided a hospital stay by volunteering to spend two days taking a battery of tests as an outpatient. Rebecca will serve as my initial escort and another friend, Gail Feinstein, will accompany me for the second day. I soon learn how essential such wonderful support from family and friends is.

In addition to the basic tests, like blood work and chest x-rays, the strength of my lungs, kidneys, liver, spleen, and vascular system will be assessed. Also required are a mammogram, Pap smear, psychiatric evaluation, and a social work interview. The work-up will culminate with a MUGGA (Resting Radionuclide Angiogram) test, a right-heart catheterization to verify the severity of my condition, and justify my listing on the United Network for Organ Sharing (UNOS) Registry, and determine if the pressures in my coronary arteries will sustain a new heart. Transplant workups are necessary because donated organs are scarce, precious, and cannot be wasted. Evidence of any kind of cancer, weak kidneys, or a problematic liver could render me ineligible. National requirements also include sound psychological health, as well as family and social support.

When we arrive, Rebecca and I check the schedule. Luckily, the times for the first four tests are sequenced so we will have an opportunity for a nice lunch

25

afterward. Despite the seriousness of it all, we try to see the humor in every aspect of the medical scrutiny.

The last appointment is for a psychiatric evaluation with Dr. Martin Whitehead. We arrive and wait more than 45 minutes before I peer at my watch and realize the nice, leisurely lunch is looking less likely. Suddenly Rebecca chuckles and elbows me. "I bet you a great lunch that that twerp over there will be filling in as your shrink." I look around and see a kid who resembles many of the college students I teach.

"You're kidding," I reply. "An intern?" Rebecca is right. Yet I cannot believe a child half my age is going to determine if I am mentally fit to have a heart transplant.

"Ms. Coleman?" he calls out.

"That's Dr. Coleman," I snap back. I am angry. No one should have to wait on anyone that long without an explanation. He neither offers one nor an apology. He leads me to a private conference room where he spends the first few minutes detailing his credentials and explaining that he will administer a mental fitness test. Questions like "What day is today?" and "Who is the President of the United States?" would be followed by more difficult questions. Doctors often want to establish a baseline so that if someone has a seizure or stroke in the hospital, they have some idea of the patient's basic mental capacity. As the young intern moves on to more complex questions, he poses them incorrectly and I correct him. Luckily, the attending physician finally enters the room and plucks this young man from the psychological rapids he is drowning in. Apparently, he has never interviewed a psychology professor about her mental toughness. The attending physician quickly sizes up the situation and gets to the point. "Are you or have you ever been suicidal?" he asks.

As with most life-threatening illnesses, recovering from a transplant is a rugged walk. Mental toughness is required, and if I don't possess it initially, I will have to develop it quickly. Suicide is not an option no matter how physically ill I feel. Having a transplant is about extending life not ending it.

The heart transplant workup is frightening. Scheduling it makes the transplant more tangible. What if I don't pass all of the exams? What if there's something wrong with me that I don't know about? What if I'm rejected? Then what? Am I doomed to die and this workup is the beginning of the terrorizing end? I think this might be a great time to talk with my heart again.

LERITA: Hi.

HEART: Hello.

LERITA: Ready to talk again?

HEART: Do I have a choice?

LERITA: Yes, we can talk later.

HEART: No, right now is OK. I am dreading this conversation.

LERITA: Why? I thought now that we're talking we are getting along better.

HEART: Is that what you think?

LERITA: Look I tried to follow your advice. I didn't push as much. I lightened things up.

HEART: Not bad for a beginner.

LERITA: I don't merit anything better than "not bad"?

HEART: Hold it. There you go being evaluative and competitive. What if you were healing from a broken leg and you knew that it would take at least six weeks for the bone to heal. Would you say after the first week, "Hey bone why aren't you healing faster?" Take a chill pill, Lerita. Nothing happens with you where you're not as tight as a new rubber band.

LERITA: OK. But I tried to be better.

HEART: Yes. You didn't push as much, and you gave me a little time to rest and relax. You took time to do nothing for a change, something you rarely do.

LERITA: Didn't I sit in bed and watch television a couple of nights?

HEART: But weren't you doing two or three other things at the same time?

LERITA: Two or three other things?

HEART: Yes, like balancing the checkbook and reading a book while watching television. Multi-tasking. Can you focus on one thing at a time?

LERITA: Please don't scream at me.

27

HEART: I'm not screaming. Alright, I'm sorry. We'll work on focus later. Let's get back to your progress. Yes, you did well, but there is some room for improvement.

LERITA: How so?

HEART: Why is it that you have to squeeze in one more thing at the end of the day?

LERITA: There are a lot of things to do.

HEART: Can't some of them wait until the next day?

LERITA: The list is so long.

HEART: Lerita, the list is endless. There are always things to do in life. There is always something to fix in the house. There is always someplace to go. You must have priorities, and I think health should be at the top of your list right now. Actually, it should be at the top of the list all of the time. Taking good care of you is what recovery is all about. How can you keep up this hectic schedule and heal at the same time?

LERITA: This is too hard; all of this heart and healing stuff. I've been struggling physically all of my life.

HEART: All the more reason why you need to make changes now.

LERITA: OK.

HEART: I know you cannot change 40 or more years of bad habits overnight or in a couple of weeks. How about taking it one day at a time?

LERITA: (Sighing) All right where do I start?

HEART: I notice that each night you seem to focus on what you didn't accomplish instead of what you did. Why is the glass always half empty?

LERITA: I don't know. I guess I think I never do enough.

HEART: How sad. A little satisfaction would go a long way. It's a bad habit, and it certainly causes a lot of stress and strain on me. Be grateful for the good day you had instead of checking to see what didn't get crossed off the list.

LERITA: Sorry.

HEART: You've got great enthusiasm and energy but you never let up.

LERITA: I need more time.

HEART: More time? You don't know how to manage the time you have now.

LERITA: Excuse me! I think I manage time quite well.

HEART: So that's why you think you need more of it?

LERITA: There are so many things to do.

HEART: You mentioned too many things to do again. Don't you see the problem? It's not more time that you need. You might give some thought to cutting down on the activities, tasks and obligations. Maybe we can get you a personal trainer, in time management that is, one of those life coaches.

LERITA: I don't need a coach. I need to figure out what I could eliminate.

HEART: Certainly anything that doesn't enrich your life.

LERITA: All I do now is work, sleep, and eat.

HEART: The work seems a little out of balance. Talking on the phone absorbs a lot of work and pleasure time.

LERITA: Are you saying I talk too much?

HEART: That's an understatement. Maybe you ought to keep a time log of your day. Then you could see how you spend your time and which parts are devoted to things that are not life-giving, energy leaks if you will.

LERITA: For a heart, you seem a little harsh. I thought I had cut back.

HEART: Lerita, I am sorry that I am not as kind and nurturing as you would like. But you need to know two things. First, our lives are on the line, and there's no time for dilly-dallying around. Second, do you realize that as your heart, I represent *your* style—direct and to the point? Compassion is not one of your strong suits. Hopefully, you will develop plenty of empathy on this next segment of the journey. Back to the daily schedule—I think you're making progress. Unfortunately, you spend an enormous amount of time worrying.

LERITA: Whoa, wait a minute. I can hardly keep up. You were commenting on my personality, and I was thinking that I can work on my compassion, but now, you're on to worry. Worrying about what?

HEART: Whatever you think up. You worry about work, and you spend an enormous amount of time worrying about me. Not that I don't like the attention. However, worrying isn't going to cure what ails me. You worry about your car, money, what others think of you, what your body looks like, how your hair is styled, how your office and house look. Should I continue?

LERITA: No that's enough

HEART: It makes me tired.

LERITA: I don't know any other way to be. Isn't there always something to worry about?

HEART: "Ye of little faith." Where's the faith you say you have in God? I thought you were supposed to be *so* spiritual.

LERITA: I *am* spiritual.

HEART: It's certainly hard to tell.

LERITA: Oh come on!

HEART: How can you say you have so much faith and you spend so much time worrying?

LERITA: Having relentless, undying faith is extremely difficult.

HEART: I understand. Letting go of some of that worrying—or better yet, cultivating some trust—would help me tremendously. We would both feel better without so much anxiety.

LERITA: Now I have anxiety! Okay, yes I feel anxious, but the docs are talking HEART TRANSPLANT. I mean they want to take you, my heart, out and put someone else's in. I'd say that is something to be concerned about, don't you think? Anything else?

HEART: There's plenty, but we can't address it all now. On the dietary side, thanks for cutting back on the salt. That helps keep me from failing.

LERITA: Yes. I understand that water retention caused by the salty food can precipitate that. So now I should...

HEART: Continue not pushing. Save some things for tomorrow. Don't beat yourself up at night. Instead of focusing on what you didn't accomplish, pat yourself on the back for what you completed. Please, utilize your spiritual resources like prayer, meditation, and nature to cultivate greater trust in your Creator instead of worrying.

LERITA: Is that it? For a diseased heart, you seem to know a lot about heart failure, emotions and spirituality. How is that?

HEART: Lerita, you will learn, as we talk further, that your heart serves as a physical pump, a container for all of your emotions and a conduit for the Spirit. It's a lot to explain tonight and we are both fatigued. Let's talk again real soon. I'll share a few more tips on healing. Remember, it starts with your mind.

LERITA: I still cannot believe I am talking to my heart and you have all of this information. What about my mind?

HEART: The healing begins in your mind with your thoughts. You're the psychologist.

LERITA: You're kind of a smart-ass.

HEART: Lerita, I wouldn't use those terms, but, if you must know, every part of you has intelligence. If you would *listen* more—especially to your body, and more specifically your "heart"—you'd discover a lot.

LERITA: Okay. That gives me a lot to ponder. Thanks.

HEART: No problem.

Reflections

What would your heart have to say about your current lifestyle?

How would your heart describe your personality?

What steps (e.g., diet, exercise, spiritual practice) do you engage in to maintain a healthy heart?

The Race for the Gold

"Kato, Kato. It looks like the transplant is a go," I shout into the phone to my closest friend of nearly 20 years.

"Oh, no, Lerita. This can't be happening," Kato says as he begins to sob.

" Get a grip, Kato. Besides, you're supposed to be comforting me."

"I know, I know. But I can't think about living without you, Lerita. How would I be able to maneuver through the world?"

"You were doing pretty well before we met. It's going to be okay."

I cannot believe that I am reassuring my friend, Kato Johnson. When we are hanging out together, people often wonder if we are married. Among the people who know us, they frequently ask when we might settle down. What most people don't know is that Kato is gay. Marriage for us is not an option. Yet we have been through so much together; my earlier heart surgery, his medical school applications, my tenure trials, his boards, and of course countless relationships. Kato often says we are twin souls. I'm not quite sure what that means, but I know that we would miss each other terribly if I died.

"The transplant workup is completed," I advised. "The doctors say that I should probably go on the list immediately, but I think I want to wait until after the holidays. The last thing I want is to have a heart transplant on Christmas Eve or Christmas Day. You know that could happen given the number of accidents that occur around the holidays."

Kato agrees. "You need the Christmas holidays to spend time with your family. Lerita, how could this be happening?" he says, trying to hold back more tears.

This scenario is becoming far too common. Shocked friends and relatives frequently start to weep when I tell them that I am going to need a heart transplant. I wonder if they think I am going to die or turn into some kind of Frankenstein. I guess most people still aren't sure what to expect.

After talking with Kato, I stumble toward the bed. I am so exhausted. Fatigue overshadows my daily schedule. I try to ignore it, but it makes its presence known like an unwanted visitor. I am unwilling to accept that I am frequently in and out of heart failure. Walking more than two blocks presents a problem, and nothing rejuvenates me. I am *always* tired and feel I carry the weariness of the world on my shoulders.

Usually, when I come in from work, I fall asleep fully clothed on one of the window seats in my living room. The naps help but living alone does not. How is dinner going to get cooked? If I fail to eat, I will have even less energy. Chicken potpies become standard fare.

I observe, too, that I suffer from immobilization. I have trouble getting up and going in the mornings. I wonder if my veil of denial is slipping away, making my morning routine so tedious? It is not only my physical deterioration that drags me down: I want to escape. I don't want to face this life and the challenges that lie ahead. I don't want to think about pills, medical procedures, and medical bills. In fact, I hate hospitals, doctors, and medications. I feel like I am on a river raft, hanging over the edge of a crest. I paddle relentlessly. What will happen if I go over the edge? Will I live? Will I ever be able to coast and take in some of the scenery? I pray, I cry. I listen. A voice is whispering to me. "You're on a diuretic. Take some potassium." My heart *is* talking to me.

LERITA: Hello? Heart, are you still there?

HEART: Now that's a ridiculous question. You wouldn't be talking to me if I weren't here.

LERITA: Hey, I was trying to start out on the light side. Do you have an attitude this morning or what?

HEART: I'm so tired all of the time now. You know how it is when you don't get enough rest. I'm irritable.

LERITA: Tell me about it. Does that mean you're going to leave? I cannot believe I am about to lose my heart.

HEART: I didn't say all that. I said I am tired this morning. You know you put in some long days.

LERITA: Well I have slowed down like you suggested. I haven't been pushing as much. I take naps. I am behind at work, and I am not worrying about it.

HEART: Not worrying? You? Not hardly.

LERITA: I am getting better don't you think?

HEART: Yes, you are doing better, Lerita, but you still have some hot spots.

LERITA: Hotspots? Where? What?

HEART: Look at your response to my comment. You need to address some of that perfectionism. And, well, you're very competitive.

LERITA: Me?

HEART: Yes, you. You are much better than you used to be. Thank goodness for good therapy and some maturity. I can remember when if you weren't the top student in a class you would go ballistic.

LERITA: What are you talking about? I was never the top student in any of my classes in high school, college or graduate school.

HEART: But you wanted to be. Besides, if you weren't at the top, you were always in the top ten percent.

LERITA: I don't think so.

HEART: Lerita, you can lie to yourself if you like, but I know the truth. You had to be competitive to get into college and to go to Harvard for graduate school. You don't need to maintain that level of competition now that you have tenure. Can you let it go?

LERITA: You think I am still competitive?

HEART: Not in the same way. When you think of your colleagues or other professional women, I know part of you constantly compares, checks to see if you are better, superior. You always want to be the best person in the room.

LERITA: What's wrong with that?

HEART: It's stressful. It's OK to be you. You are one of a kind. I reminded you in our first conversation that you are extraordinary. Why can't you accept the talents of others?

LERITA: What do you mean?

HEART: Every time you hear that a psychology professor, especially a former classmate or former student, publishes something, your blood pressure rises. Each time some contemporary black intellectual or any woman writes a book, there is something about their accomplishments that eats at you like a parasite.

LERITA: I don't think like that.

HEART: You like the state of denial, don't you? C'mon. Each time you listen to that radio program you like so much on NPR—what is it, *Air Fresheners*?

LERITA: *Fresh Air*. I thought you knew everything.

HEART: Major things about you, yes. Some of the minor details are fuzzy.

LERITA: You're talking about the program that interviews writers and discusses the books they have published.

HEART: Yes. Yes.

LERITA: Terry Gross interviews more than writers on the show. She talks to musicians, film directors, actors and writers, political activists, and community workers.

HEART: Right.

LERITA: Right what?

HEART: Among that group of people, whose accomplishments irk you the most?

LERITA: Irk me?

HEART: Spare me, Lerita. Is it because you feel you haven't achieved enough or that you think other people are getting ahead of you in the race for the gold?

LERITA: The race for the gold?

HEART: Yes. Isn't that the ultimate in worldly competition, like winning a gold medal in the Olympics?

LERITA: Yes, although I've not thought about being in the Olympics.

HEART: I see we're back in denial. How many times have you watched the Olympics and wished you were there competing for a gold medal?

LERITA: OK, so I've wished I could go, but I knew it was impossible because, uh, well, you know...

HEART: Go on and say it, Lerita. Because you have a "bad heart."

LERITA: I didn't want to hurt your feelings.

HEART: (Chuckling) You're going to tell your heart that you didn't want to hurt its feeling. I am the *source* of feeling. Let's get back to your competitive personality.

LERITA: Oh, it's a defining characteristic?

HEART: Yes.

LERITA: All right. All right. I admit it. I like to be the best, to be better at things than most people. Yes, I want to win the race, to capture the gold.

HEART: Have you asked yourself why you are in the race?

LERITA: Hmm. You mean like what is the purpose? The goal?

HEART: Yes.

LERITA: I feel good when I win. When I best other people.

HEART: For how long?

LERITA: For a while, I guess.

HEART: And doesn't the glory wear off after a while?

LERITA: Maybe.

HEART: Let me give you a couple of examples. You eclipsed some other students to get admitted to Harvard. Do you still feel a thrill from that?

LERITA: I wouldn't call it a thrill. That was almost 15 years ago.

HEART: OK. What about that article you published in the top journal in your field last year? Are you still feeling ecstatic about that?

LERITA: Well no. I guess it's time for me to publish another one.

HEART: Don't you see? How long do you have to keep running the race? What do you do after you've won the "gold" to keep the "thrill of victory" and stave off the "agony of da-feet?"

LERITA: (Laughing) Cute.

HEART: Trust me. There's humor in everything. Besides a smile or a laugh is a wondrous thing. But we're getting off track, no pun intended. Really, when does the race end? When are you going to get off the track, get off the slope, put down the racket, get out of the pool?

LERITA: Most Olympic stars go on to other careers. Many of them are coaches.

HEART: Right. And some of them don't know when to stop competing. Some athletes are so competitive that they injure themselves playing the sport much too long. It's not necessary to keep vying for some award.

LERITA: What am I supposed to do? I think I was born competitive, and like you say, it is a part of my personality. When I see others achieving, it makes me feel inadequate, like I don't measure up or I haven't done enough.

HEART: I hope we're through with the "not done enough" phase. If you were in love with life, with what you do, you wouldn't be concerned about what others are doing or not doing.

LERITA: Sorry, I *am* driven. I feel like I'll never catch up.

HEART: Who told you that you had to be in a contest? Try to think about it in a different way. Don't be intimidated by the success of others—be *inspired*.

LERITA: Be inspired?

HEART: The success of others shows you what's possible for you. A successful person is holding the beacon that lights the path for you.

LERITA: Actually, I wish they would go away.

HEART: I see you're into the real destructive kind of competition.

LERITA: There are different kinds?

HEART: Yes, and you are stuck in the kind in which you not only want to win, you also want to eliminate the competition.

LERITA: It sounds ugly.

HEART: It *is* ugly. That mess with Tonya Harding and Nancy Kerrigan skating for the gold medal epitomized the unpleasant side of competition. There are thousands of examples of sabotage in science, business and law. And did you notice that neither one of those women won the gold?

LERITA: Yes. The woman who won was skating for her deceased mother.

HEART: You're catching on. Just remember that the best kind of competition has a selfless purpose. If you're doing something merely to garner a personal award or to add another line to your resume, or add more money to your bank account, then the "thrill is gone" before you know it.

LERITA: I think I am beginning to get it. I can't seem to let go of the competitive spirit. It feels so "un-American" not to be competitive.

HEART: It's not difficult. Remember, Nobel Prize winners usually are not *trying* to win an award. In most cases, they are doing something they love or are inspired to do. Their findings are often serendipitous. What they discover or develop is a gift to the entire world. Think of the many discoveries in science and medicine that will help you and others like you. Think of how you have been touched by beautifully written poetry or books, awe-inspiring paintings or well-crafted motion pictures. Yes, some individuals win awards and honors, but usually, they are not *trying* to. The inspiration comes from a deeper place.

LERITA: You've given me lots to think about. You're kind of heavy, aren't you?

HEART: They don't call me "Heavy Harvey" for nothing.

LERITA: (Laughing) Heavy Harvey? That's your name? I can't believe you've got a name!

HEART: What's so funny?

LERITA: You're a heart. Why do you have a name?

HEART: *You* have a name, don't you? Should I be laughing because your name is Lo-rita?

LERITA: It's spelled L-e-r-i-t-a and pronounced Loo-rita. Does every organ have a name?

HEART: Does every person have a name?

LERITA: I guess I'll have to call you by your name from here on out. Heavy Harvey—HH for short. And I can't believe what a smart mouth you have!

HH: Don't get too excited, Loo-rita. I'll have to pump harder. By the way, why is it pronounced Loo-rita instead of Lo-rita?

LERITA: It's based on the proper pronunciation of my father's name, Loo-roy, not Lee-roy

HH: My, my, my, some of you middle-class black...

LERITA: Don't even go there.

HH: All right, All right. It's just a little heart humor with an ethnic slant.

LERITA: A wisecracking heart with a name! What will I discover next?

HH: ...That things are not as bad as they appear?

LERITA: I have one more question.

HH: What is that?

LERITA: How can I be a female with a male heart?

HH: There is no such thing as a male or female heart, but I have a masculine tone.

LERITA: How can that be?

HH: Only the mind needs to categorize, Lerita. In the world of hearts, there is no such thing as gender. Haven't you noticed that a heart looks the same whether it is in a male or female body, anatomically that is?

LERITA: Well, yeah but...

HH: Hearts are universal. That's why they can be transplanted into different bodies without regard to gender, race or class.

LERITA: I can be female and have a male heart?

HH: Need I repeat myself? Your heart has a masculine *tone*. Heart issues are a lot deeper than the human mind can process. My voice sounds male, but I am not.

LERITA: If you say so.

HH: Trust me. You'll understand it better by and by. I think we need to stop here so we can get some rest.

LERITA: Yes, that would be nice. I'll look forward to talking with you next week.

HH: OK.

Reflections

Do you sometimes feel exhausted trying to keep up with all that is on your "to do" list? Are there some activities, tasks or obligations that you might give up?

Is there some way to "slow down the race," "get off the track," "put down the racket" in order to have more peace and joy in your life?

Are you competing for the glory of it, or for some higher purpose?

To Transplant or Not to Transplant?

I wish I could drop this preoccupation with my heart. Every palpitation is significant. Is it going to stop before I can have a transplant? As I look around my bedroom, I wonder if I will survive. I've replaced the basket holding my pills twice as the number of bottles increases, requiring larger baskets. I don't like medications. I am a vitamin and herb person. Then there is the green oxygen tank with the metered dial in the corner. I feel the periodic panic of a shortness of breath, of not being able to get enough air. As usual, the fatigue rolls over me like a thick fog. Yet I'm terrified to fall asleep.

Each night when I lay down to sleep, I wonder if it will be my last. If it is time to say goodbye, I want to see Mom and Dad, my brothers —Kenneth and Robert—and my sister, Nicole. I don't want to die alone in my house only to be discovered as a decomposed, stinking corpse two or three days later. I am so tired, yet I must stay awake. Despite this nightly routine of terror, I succumb to the exhaustion and fall fast asleep.

I awake to chanting. I hear it everywhere. "Transplant," "transplant," "transplant." Is it a dream or is it my heart? Despite my apprehensions, is a transplant my fate? But I don't want to have it.

The doctors see no alternative. Each time I look at the medical regimen, I equivocate. While recovering from my earlier open-heart surgery for the same wretched heart condition, I lay in the hospital thinking God must want me to live. Now I have doubts. Wasn't that first open-heart surgery enough? If I survive the transplant, I guess I will be certain that I have a life purpose to fulfill.

Dr. Thompson put it to me straight last week: Twenty years ago, they would have sent me home to die. He explained that I am doing remarkably well considering the condition of my heart. Most patients with hearts as weak as mine can barely walk across the room, and they must carry oxygen with them everywhere. At least I can dress myself, drive and slowly walk to my office from the car.

Now that I know my dying heart has a name and it sounds male, I wonder about a new heart. Will my donor be a male or female, a black person, white person, or an Asian or Latin person? Does it make a difference? If I remember correctly, the first heart transplant involved black and white South African men. Clearly, race is not a factor in determining an organ transplant donor or recipient, although many people believe that a same-race match is better. Since I live in Colorado, it is highly likely that my donor will be white. Given my history with race relations, I cannot hide my ambivalence. I have seen and experienced so much in my life from segregation to debates about affirmative action. What would it be like to have the heart of a white man beating inside of me when I struggle daily with their unspoken condescension? Growing up in Southern California, my friends came from a wide variety of racial and ethnic backgrounds. I suppose the transplant experience will be no different. How will this traumatic event alter my outlook on race?

I want to believe that everything will turn out fine but how much trust in God do I have? Forty-one seems like such a young age to die. I pray that I will be guided to make the right choice, whether it is to have a heart transplant or die. I know, though, that in order for me to live, I need some reasons to keep on keeping on.

LERITA: Yo, heart.

HH: Come on, Lerita. I know you don't talk like that.

LERITA: I thought you were my *down* heart with an ethnic slant.

HH: That's not the point. It sounds like you're trying to be somebody you aren't. Your mother didn't bring you up saying, "Hey yo."

LERITA: That sounds so elitist.

HH: Nobody is judging language or hip-hop culture here. It is not the way *you* were raised. I don't know why you think you have to act like it is. I know that you contacted me for something other than this. What's on your mind?

LERITA: I think you know.

HH: Are you avoiding something?

LERITA: This is so hard.

HH: Just spit it out. We don't have all day.

LERITA: Can't you stay?

HH: What?

LERITA: Can't you stay with me? I know the doctors are saying that a transplant is inevitable, but I am just getting to know you. I like talking with you, and I cannot imagine you not being around. I've started making the changes that you asked for like no caffeine, resting every day and slowing down.

HH: Because you are making changes in your life doesn't mean I can stay, Lerita. Tomorrow is not promised and, I might add, today isn't guaranteed either.

LERITA: We've been through so much together.

HH: My, you're getting sentimental on me. I can relate to how you feel, but we've got to keep the ultimate goal in mind.

LERITA: What is that?

HH: Life and living. Don't you want to live?

LERITA: Yeah, I guess so. I can't imagine living without you, though.

HH: Do you mean that?

LERITA: It's true. I don't want to let you go.

HH: Lerita, you could be jeopardizing your existence by trying to hold on to me. Yes, we've been through a lot together. Yet I am surprised at you. Most of the old times have been hard and tough. Hasn't it been a real struggle for you?

LERITA: Well, yes.

HH: Don't you worry about buildings without elevators? Aren't you paralyzed by sub-zero temperatures because of me, your good ol' heart? You agonize all the time about if I'm going to stop on you.

LERITA: Are you?

HH: I can't promise you that I can last as long as you. Remember, I came here with a distorted DNA code.

LERITA: So you want to retire?

HH: This decision is not about me. It's about you. You might be able to start having fun. I know you love nature walks and hikes. How would you feel with tons more energy?

LERITA: Probably out of control. I've had tons of energy. I think that is why I always feel overwhelmed.

HH: Isn't that why we're having these conversations? We can possibly eliminate some of your mental and physical anguish. I know you've always wanted to ride your bicycle to campus in the summer. I can't even get you to the end of the street. With a new heart, you might be able to enjoy life—without worrying so much about your heart.

LERITA: I guess I am still not convinced.

HH: I wasn't trying to persuade you to take me out. I was trying to give you another perspective from someone who has your best interests at heart.

LERITA: That's an awful pun. You call that a sense of humor?

HH: Only trying to get you to smile. You know you haven't been doing much of that lately. Your angst over the decision to have a transplant is heartbreaking.

LERITA: Pa-leeze.

HH: Sorry, but you're smiling.

LERITA: It's too much. I can't believe after all we've been through I would need another surgery, a transplant at that!

HH: Can we please get off that "woe is me, pity party-for-one" kick? Do you know how blessed you are?

LERITA: What is so blessed about having a heart transplant at age 41?!

HH: Sometimes I don't believe the things that come out of your mouth, Lerita. How can you *not* see the blessings in this situation? First of all, do you understand that with your insurance coverage, the transplant is completely covered except for a small deductible?

LERITA: Yeah.

HH: Don't get so excited. We're talking about a medical procedure that costs $150K at minimum. Then, you also have coverage for some very expensive medications.

LERITA: I know.

HH: Such enthusiasm. Really Lerita, you seem so ungrateful.

LERITA: Keep talking.

HH: OK. Then there are your colleagues. They are going to pitch in and teach for you. Given that you don't have much sick leave accumulated, I'd say that's a huge blessing.

LERITA: OK.

HH: What happened to that effervescent personality you carry around with you most of the time?

LERITA: Apparently it evaporated.

HH: Boy, you sure are in a funky mood today.

LERITA: It happens sometimes. Please go on.

HH: As I was saying, your colleagues have volunteered to help out. Now that's a miracle considering how difficult you claim them to be.

LERITA: It is remarkable I must admit.

HH: Then there is your family. Mom and Dad are ready to move to Colorado to take care of you when you have the transplant.

LERITA: I can't wait.

HH: I'm going to ignore your overall pitifulness, Lerita. Do you know how amazing it is for a 41-year-old woman to *have* parents who are healthy enough to come take care of *her* after major surgery, let alone the fact that they are *willing* to do so? Some parents might not want to spend their time that way, or they are too irresponsible to help. In fact, at your age, it's usually the other way around. Most people are taking care of their parents.

LERITA: OK.

HH: Should I go on about your friends, some of whom have already gone beyond the call of duty to be supportive?

LERITA: I know. I know.

HH: And the medical facilities. You've got one of the best transplant teams in the country. The aftercare is phenomenal. What more could you ask for?

LERITA: How about NOT having a transplant? How about some miraculous healing on your part?

HH: That may not be possible, Lerita. Sometimes things are out of our control—yours or mine. And just why are you so opposed to having a heart transplant?

LERITA: Where do you want me to begin?

HH: Wherever you would like to start.

LERITA: The doctors talk about having a heart transplant like it's a piece of cake. They saunter into the OR, play some nice music, take out your old heart and sew another one in. From the way they talk, you would think they were sewing a lining in a dress.

HH: Well the doctor did say it is a fairly simple operation.

LERITA: Right. That was a cardiologist talking, not a surgeon. Besides, unlike any of them, I have had open-heart surgery. I've been in the operating room having them put the mask on my face. I've awakened in ICU with nearly every part of my body connected to something. It's not pretty.

HH: I can understand that, however...

LERITA: Then there is the medical maintenance. If I have a transplant, I have to have several mini-heart catheterizations, which they call right heart biopsies. I hate heart catheterizations. I've hated them since I had my first one at age 11. God forbid the immune suppressant medications I have to take for life. Then I have to start worrying about infections, rejection and God knows what else.

HH: Worrying? I thought we addressed that earlier.

LERITA: We may have addressed it, but we didn't cure it.

HH: Could it be that if you had perfect trust, there would be no worry?

LERITA: Perfect trust? Come on.

HH: Complete surrender to something more powerful than either of us?

LERITA: If I had perfect trust, probably neither one of us would be on the planet, and we certainly wouldn't be having *this* conversation. Since when did *you* start being so spiritual?

HH: Since it seemed you lost your faith because I got ill. You know, you tend to have lots of faith until something bad happens. Are you sure you're not a pessimist at heart?

LERITA: This is definitely no time for *that* pun. If you are correct, Mr. Smarty Pants, why do you seem more optimistic than I am?

HH: Because I am a symbolic representation of your physical and emotional heart, which you have chosen to anthropomorphize?

LERITA: (Laughing) Are you trying to ridicule my scholarly language?

HH: (Laughing) I am the voice of *your* heart, remember? I may not always share your sentiments. I am here to help you to know your true feelings and to share with you messages from your spirit. You can have a funky attitude, but it may not be what your heart genuinely feels.

LERITA: I don't understand all of that, and we digress. Let's get back to the terror.

HH: Right—the terror.

LERITA: Are you being sarcastic again?

HH: No. Remember, I don't necessarily share your terror. Please go on.

LERITA: I don't like to be sick, and the thought of complications frightens me. There are side effects to the medications. Thinking about it makes me tremble. It's all compounded by my fear of dying.

HH: Fear of dying?

LERITA: Not dying during the operation. Having a transplant makes me think about having a finite, countable number of years remaining on the earth. I hope for 25 or 30 more years at the minimum, although that's less likely if I have a heart transplant. I guess we are all dying, but I don't have to think about it when I am healthy and well. By having a heart transplant, dying is not a someday proposition. It feels closer, like next month, or next year, or in five years.

HH: You've hit the nail on the head. Why are you thinking about dying so much? Why are you so focused on what could go wrong?

47

LERITA: Listen. You're talking to a long-standing, card-carrying optimist, Pollyanna in her prime. Label it unrealistic optimism. Some friends say I could have given Norman Vincent Peale some competition.

HH: What happened?

LERITA: Bad things happened.

HH: According to your perception? Things happen. How about not judging them as "good" or "bad"? What do you think has happened?

LERITA: I guess life hasn't turned out like I had expected.

HH: Welcome to life, Miss Lerita. Who do you think feels like life turned out like they expected? Have you thought about letting go of some of your expectations?

LERITA: How can I do that?

HH: I think we may need to save that topic for another conversation. Don't you think we've talked long enough today?

LERITA: Not really. Can I go on?

HH: If you must.

LERITA: Maybe I need the transplant.

HH: Oh?

LERITA: I don't think I have a choice. They completed the transplant workup and that's the recommendation. We know what the alternative is. I mean isn't a transplant looking pretty inevitable?

HH: Yes, it is Lerita. You'll do fine.

LERITA: I'm so angry with my body. I feel like it betrayed me.

HH: Betrayed you?

LERITA: Yeah, especially when I have to take all of these medications.

HH: You think *I* betrayed you?

LERITA: I knew you were sick all along. I always tried to quietly tiptoe around you. I participated in the physical activities that I could but I've filled my life with different, more intellectual stuff that doesn't require too much exertion. Now I need a transplant. It involves so much!

HH: What's involved?

LERITA: First, there are the costs. How am I going to pay for medicines that have co-pays of $1,600 per month the first year and $500 per month for the rest of my life? I've worked so hard to have a beautiful home, and to pay my bills and most of my savings will be wiped out in the first year. Then, every one of the medications has side effects. I don't know how I'm going to do it (sobbing).

HH: I wish I could be more sympathetic Lerita. On the contrary, have you ever had any trouble paying for medication?

LERITA: No.

HH: Let me try to put it this way, Lerita—bluntly. Your grandfather died from this same disease 25 years ago. Then, they neither had the operation nor the medications.

LERITA: I see your point. I need to see the blessing behind it all.

HH: We definitely needed this conversation.

LERITA: I still don't like taking medications.

HH: OK, Lerita. Why don't you like taking medications?

LERITA: I went over that already. When I take medications, I feel defeated. I feel deficient.

HH: Defeated by what? Deficient in what way?

LERITA: Hmm. I guess by my body. It's like it is out of control, extraneous to me. I don't know what it will do or how much pain I will have to endure or if I might die. When I have to take a lot of medications, I feel like I have lost the battle with my body. It's like going into the hospital. I'll do anything to avoid it. I know as soon as I walk through the doors, I have lost control over my body. I hate it.

HH: So the real issue here is about control, huh Lerita? You want to control everything.

LERITA: Not everything, just my body.

49

HH: Let's get back to the real issue.

LERITA: Yes, the medications.

HH: No, control.

LERITA: It's not about medications?

HH: Can't you see, Lerita? You want to direct everything and everybody. You even want to direct your own healing.

LERITA: It's scary not knowing what is going to happen, I mean I cannot predict the future and...

HH: Uncertainty pervades the world, and there are many things that you cannot control, Lerita. Things happen to people every day; fires, floods, hurricanes and tornadoes. Your situation may seem unusual, but it's just another uncontrollable event.

LERITA: Just another uncontrollable event? Did you notice that all of the situations you named are bad?

HH: Depends on your perspective. Good things happen to people too, and they often emerge after catastrophes.

LERITA: Like what?

HH: Like heart transplants! Lerita, do you know anything about surrender, about letting go?

LERITA: Surrender? Doesn't that sound like defeat to you? In a battle, when you surrender, it means the other side won.

HH: In a battle? Is this a war with your body, with me, your heart? By the way, in law, surrender means "restoration of an estate." Think about that. You might gain by surrendering to this heart transplant.

LERITA: Gain what?

HH: A whole new life?

LERITA: Really?

HH: Lerita you like running everything. Can you understand why I am so tired? For the most part, you've performed well. But try listening and letting go. Let go of this transplant. Let go of the anxiety about medications. Remember the key word here is TRUST. If you trust, you'll be fine. If you try to control everything, you're doomed for sure.

LERITA: Doomed, as in, die?

HH: No, more like in needless suffering. Trust the little Voice, the one that is deeper than mine. I know you are familiar with "the still small voice" that is from Spirit within. I think you'll be a lot happier.

LERITA: I'll try.

HH: Look, we have a little more time before I have to say good-bye and your new heart arrives. Let's work on your attitudes about the medications, otherwise, it's going to be tough. Remember, there has to be some reason why you were born in a time when transplants are available instead of 25 years ago when you would have died. Be thankful for the technological advances that allow you to have a transplant and medications that will prevent you from rejecting a new heart.

LERITA: OK, so you'll still be here next week?

HH: Sure. I'll let you know when it is time to say goodbye.

LERITA: Alright. We'll talk next week.

Reflections

Has there ever been a situation in your life where you exhibited perfect trust? Can you describe what that felt like?

Describe a traumatic experience whose blessings were only apparent later?

Can you list your reasons for living?

Packing Resentments

The shock of a potential heart transplant remains with me. I am angry because I cannot believe that I am going to have open-heart surgery *again*. Once is enough. I thought that I was cured after open-heart surgery 14 years ago. For many heart recipients, the transplant is the first time for surgery. I know, though, what it means to wake up in ICU with wires and tubes all over the place.

I also know what it feels like to have scars on my body. I stand in front of the mirror and wonder if the surgeon will follow the same lines of the old scar that is now a keloid. As I trace these scars with my fingers, I think back to my clinic visit today. I asked the transplant coordinator if I could speak with a transplant surgeon to discuss how the multiple scars will look on my chest. Surprisingly, she chided me for being concerned. "I have a 16-year-old patient who has high self-esteem. She has no problems with having a scar. Besides, you are getting a new heart," she noted. I think first about the young 16-year-old girl who has no idea what a scar on her chest means yet.

Then I ask myself, "Why does everyone think that having a transplant is *only* about being grateful, as if nothing else mattered?" I know the transplant coordinator did not have a clue about what another scar might mean to a 41-year-old single woman who, as a professor, stands in front of an audience two to three times a week; about what type of bathing suit I could wear at the beach or kind of dress for an evening gown? At least my previous surgeon was thoughtful enough to give me what he described as a "champagne cut" (cut in the shape of a champagne glass), so I wouldn't be relegated to turtlenecks for the rest of my life. Having another scar on my chest *is* important to me. I felt crushed when the surgeon informed me that they would have to cut both above and below my present incision to take my old heart out and put the new one in. When I arrived home, I sat down among the many scooped neck summer and cocktail dresses in my closet and sobbed.

Tonight I ponder so many more questions and concerns that haven't been addressed by the transplant team. Will I be able to have romantic relationships after the transplant? What kind of sex life will I have? I might not have enough energy or any libido. If the transplant medications are anything like heart failure drugs, so long sexual desire and orgasms. How am I going to tell a man that I've had a heart transplant? Will it scare him away? Why is there no one I can talk to about these issues? I cannot ask the doctors because none of them are transplant recipients. The questions seem much too personal to ask any of the older transplant recipients I've met who serve as mentors.

I remember my first boyfriend, Jonathan, informing me shortly after I met him that he felt I was too sickly for him. He wanted to explore the outdoors, and he didn't think I could keep up. Of course, I thought he could have kept those comments to himself, but at least he was honest. Other guys don't call back, or they slither away after they hear the news about my heart. Some blurt out inappropriately, "Does that mean that you cannot have kids?" I wish I had a husband, but I guess that is no guarantee either. I've heard horror stories about patients whose spouses have left either before or after the transplant. They say they cannot handle it or the experience is too intense. The resentment bubbles up again as I ruminate about this major disruption to my life.

LERITA: Hello?

HH: (No answer)

LERITA: Hello? My dear heart, are you still there?

HH: (No answer)

LERITA: Heavy, HEAVY HARVEY, ARE YOU THERE?

HH: Oh hi. Sorry, I was packing.

LERITA: You were what?

HH: Packing, packing my suitcase. Why are you acting so surprised?

LERITA: The transplant is getting to be so real. I mean you really *are* leaving, huh?

HH: Yes, but I thought we got that sorted out already. Are you having second thoughts?

LERITA: Does it matter?

HH: What's with the sarcasm?

LERITA: I'm sorry. I guess that every time I think of you leaving, being gone forever, I get shivers up and down my spine. I know it's happening, but I guess it still seems surreal.

HH: Lerita, how can I say this gently? I think you need to get with the program. The transplant is going to happen. Are you ready?

LERITA: Well, I guess so. I have so many things to do.

HH: Have you made a list? You know you are great at making lists.

LERITA: Yes, but I haven't gotten very far with accomplishing the tasks on the list.

HH: What's left to do?

LERITA: I've got to pack my bags ... Oh, I get it. That's why you are packing too.

HH: Lerita, I know you are sharper than this. Of course, I am packing my bags. Remember, I have to be ready to go too.

LERITA: By the way, I know what I'm packing. I've got a good novel, my pajamas, my teddy bear, my living will, slippers, journal, and a notebook. But what are *you* packing?

HH: Good question. What do you think I am packing?

LERITA: What do you mean?

HH: Are there some things that I should take with me, things that may be sitting in your heart?

LERITA: That's a deep question.

HH: Thanks, but that's what hearts are known for—dealing with the *deep* stuff. It is the place from which much wisdom emerges. Still, I consider it a special compliment since you have blamed me for your God-awful life.

LERITA: Yeah, well, I regret that. It's hard to balance the good and bad. My lifelong struggle with a heart problem represents the bad part. The good part is that you are so wise and you've tried to help me.

HH: Oh yeah?

LERITA: What if my new heart isn't as smart and wise as you are?

HH: First, you need to understand that all hearts are wise. Beneath all of the emotional stuff lies your beautiful and pure heart. It is the source of the wisdom that comes through when your heart isn't so clogged up with emotional baggage. Sometimes you think you are listening to it, but you aren't. You are listening to your ego and neediness instead. But let's save that discussion for another time. I want to get back to what you think I ought to pack in my suitcase.

LERITA: OK. What should you take? You're not coming back, I mean, not coming back home with me.

HH: That's right. What can I take with me that you may not want to bring back home with your new heart?

LERITA: I'm not sure what you mean.

HH: Lerita, if you could take something from your heart, something that you know you want to let go of once and for all, what would it be? Is there anything weighing down your heart?

LERITA: More great questions. Let's see … Yes, I *am* carrying some things in my heart. Too bad I have to have this damn transplant—that you have to leave for me to let go of them permanently.

HH: Hey, let's not get upset about the transplant again. It's a blessing.

LERITA: I understand that. I'm scared.

HH: My heart goes out to you.

LERITA: Not another pun?

HH: I'm sorry I couldn't resist. See there, you're smiling again.

LERITA: I guess I harbor some resentment about racism and sexism. I hate it when people hate or devalue a person they don't know for no other reason than that they look different or they are different culturally or ethnically or because that person is a woman.

HH: How is hating racism and sexism going to help the situation? Aren't you perpetuating it by hating it?

LERITA: How could I be adding to the problem?

HH: Anger and resentment, even hatred, are nothing but energy, and that energy can be destructive, instructive or constructive.

LERITA: Right, and press one for more options. Gimme a break. How can it be all three?!

HH: Now, now. You're starting to raise your voice.

LERITA: Sometimes your answers are...

HH: You're getting a little hotheaded. Patience, Lerita, you've got to develop more patience. This is not a race. It's a conversation.

LERITA: OK.

HH: As I was saying, the energy derived from anger can be used destructively to hurt or harm someone, but you can also learn from it and put it to good use. I've seen you do all three with the same incident. Remember when Ronnie Rodgers...

LERITA: Stop right there. You do not have to recount that sordid situation. Yes, and if I had had a gun, I would have shot him. I didn't know I could feel that much rage.

HH: You learned a lot from that encounter, didn't you?

LERITA: Yes, I did. I never imagined that I would meet a man who had two other girlfriends at the same time. In these days and times, that is so dangerous. I trusted him—well sort of. I had that sixth sense that he wasn't altogether trustworthy, but I didn't want to believe it. I truly wanted to believe that he was Mr. Right.

HH: If you had only listened to me. I sent as many red flags as I could. Thank God you put that rage to good use. Isn't that when you started writing on a regular basis? Wasn't it a constructive way to vent that anger? Think about how many people you've touched with your writing.

LERITA: Getting those feelings on paper helped a lot.

HH: See, a constructive use of anger.

LERITA: Isn't sexism different?

HH: Thoughts and feelings are pretty powerful, especially in their effects on the body. Your thoughts of resentment are not hurting anyone besides you, especially your mind and organs. Negative and hate thoughts produce different biochemical reactions than caring and loving thoughts. Loving thoughts enhance healing.

LERITA: But I am affected by the condescension and disrespect I receive from men. I feel slighted, angry and unworthy.

HH: Yes, but the feelings only affect you if you believe them. You are judging yourself when that happens, Lerita. You are your worst enemy.

LERITA: That's possibly true, but...

HH: You've read the material out there on healing. People with positive attitudes, people who are optimistic, people with hope and faith, and who are full of love, recover much faster from surgery and a host of illnesses than people who are carrying around a lot of anger and resentment.

LERITA: Then what am I supposed to do? Continue to let men discriminate against me or expect me to take care of them, but rarely lift a finger to care for me?

HH: A man can only disrespect you if you allow him. Usually, you are too timid to speak up. That is where the disrespect comes in. You're afraid that you'll never meet another man or that your boss will always be male and control your destiny. Don't give all of your power away to other people, especially men, by investing your energy in the wrong place—in fear. I am not telling you to ignore your feelings, but you already know you deserve to be cherished. Remember these words, Lerita. *"Teach," "healthy boundaries"* and *"forgiveness."*

LERITA: (Sarcastically) Right.

HH: Listen to your tone of voice. Don't jump to conclusions.

LERITA: All right.

HH: You teach people how to treat you. Are you speaking primarily about your romantic relationships?

LERITA: Mostly, although, as you know, my workplace is full of male professors. Their competitive energy is often stifling.

HH: Dominance is a common attribute of spirits who think of themselves as males, Lerita. You have to forgive them. That is how men are socialized in many cultures, and they frequently believe that being a man means being better than a woman. Some of them lose that ego-based need for power as they mature.

LERITA: So I have to live with disdain and discrimination?

HH: First, assert yourself, like I mentioned. Set some healthy boundaries. Let people know what is acceptable and what isn't acceptable to you. Do you get angry with children because they are too young to know the rules? No, you teach them by modeling the appropriate behavior. Racist and sexist people, and they come in both genders, are like children. They are ignorant, feel extremely insecure, unworthy, and do not know who they are. Also, their hearts are packed with fear. That's why they need other people to attack or devalue so their own self-esteem is bolstered temporarily. Have mercy and compassion for them, but don't let them determine how *you* feel about yourself.

LERITA: They know the rules; they know I'm a person.

HH: Think of them as *spiritually asleep*. They're only aware of social mores, not the universal laws, otherwise, they would never insult or mistreat another human being for any reason. When you attack someone, you're attacking yourself. What goes around comes around. You get that in Basic Spirituality 101. That's why it's so important to deal with grievances as they arise. Besides, you can turn that humiliation and resentment into something constructive by using the energy of anger and resentment to perfect your craft.

LERITA: Perfect my craft?

HH: Yes. You love to write.

LERITA: Yes. But I need to write about every experience?

HH: Maybe I'm being too vague. You can channel that anger by coming home and perfecting a paragraph or editing a few pages of one of your books.

LERITA: Not everyone is a writer, Heavy. What do people who aren't writers do?

HH: Each person is blessed with some gift or talent, although most people aren't always aware of what their gift is. Perfecting a talent or gift requires daily practice, though. It's like practicing the piano or training for a race. Having a heart transplant is a very traumatic experience, but doing something creative with your feelings of fear and anxiety by writing about them is healing. Don't they have some technical term for that?

LERITA: There's the Freudian term, sublimation. Any negative experience or impulse or negative emotion can be transformed into something positive. Then there is expanding research on post-traumatic growth.

HH: Yes, positive and useful. Remember what Duke Ellington said, "I merely took the energy it takes to pout and wrote some blues." Look at the wonderful music he created. One day others will read our dialogues and be strengthened, inspired and encouraged by them. Similar to when you read a book that speaks to you. It's a chain.

LERITA: Hmm. A chain. What about people who haven't discovered their talents?

HH: Then they should devote their energy to discerning what their gifts are.

LERITA: How do they do that?

HH: It's not difficult, Lerita. It's about knowing what makes your heart sing.

LERITA: Is that another pun?

HH: No. I am very serious. What brings you joy? What makes you come alive? Haven't you heard that famous quote by the African-American mystic and theologian, Howard Thurman? He says, "Don't ask yourself what the world needs. Ask what makes you come alive and then go do that. Because what the world needs is people who have come alive."

LERITA: I'm not familiar with Howard Thurman, but I like the concept. What brings joy to my heart? Let's see. I love flowers. Shasta daisies, zinnias, dahlias growing in my yard make my heart sing. I love writing, sewing and fabric, and I love reading. I guess there are other things, but that's the short list.

HH: How did you determine that those things bring you joy?

LERITA: Oh I don't know. I was sitting around one day thinking about what I loved to do as a child. I reminisced about my favorite pastimes and how I had lost my connection with them by becoming a workaholic and leading a fast-paced life. I discovered a lot of peace and tranquility when I returned to the activities I loved as a child.

HH: It's that simple. Your talents are in gardening, writing, sewing, and reading. I suspect you could have chosen any one of those vocations and been successful. Being a great gardener makes a marvelous contribution. In fact, I know your friends and neighbors love your beautiful flowers. And you have made enough clothes to have your own fashion boutique. Had you not become a professor and writer, you might have become a fashion designer or worked in retail and merchandising.

LERITA: How could I make a contribution to the world by becoming a fashion designer?

HH: Every task performed with *love* in your heart spreads joy. Don't you feel good when you wear gorgeous clothes? Doesn't a person in beautiful clothes make you feel happy?

LERITA: Is it the clothes?

HH: No, it's not the clothes, it's the energy of love behind their creation. It's similar to walking away from a great theater production, movie or concert. Don't you feel uplifted when you leave?

LERITA: If it is phenomenal—like *The Phantom of the Opera* or an August Wilson play or jazz musicians like Grover Washington, Jr., Rachelle Ferrell, Kevin Mahogany, Tony Bennett or Nancy Wilson. Yes, I feel exhilarated.

HH: That is what I am talking about. It is not solely about music or art. You can feel good working with an outstanding lawyer, doctor or businessperson. Hell, a person collecting garbage with love is making a contribution by keeping the world clean and free of disease and rodents. I tell you, every *loving* act is a gift. But it's only a contribution if it is carried out with love.

LERITA: Why does it have to be conducted with love?

HH: Doing things, yet secretly being resentful, blocks the energy force of love. You can tell when someone is doing something half-heartedly or with an angry heart. It is not the same as someone doing exactly the same task with love. You know that quilt you have in the guest bedroom?

LERITA: The hand-made one that Great Aunt Lucy in Texas sent me?

HH: Yes, don't you feel the love each time you touch or look at it?

LERITA: You're right, Heavy, I do. The feeling of love intensifies every time I think about all of the time and care she put into making that quilt—every single stitch was hand sewn. In fact, when I feel I need some love and nurturing, I wrap myself inside of it.

HH: That's what I mean when I say the energy is different in things made with love or given from love. It carries a special kind of energy that nurtures and heals.

LERITA: How fascinating.

HH: It's how life is. Unfortunately, you've blocked a lot of your good because you've carried so much resentment and contempt for men in your heart, Lerita.

LERITA: I am still worried about women and girls suffering all over the world. I think about the women in my family, including me, who take care of so much. The work is endless.

HH: If you don't ask for what you need, you won't get what you want.

LERITA: Easier said than done, Heavy.

HH: You don't have to make every guy you meet a home cooked meal because you're trying to "catch him." Why don't you observe what he's bringing to the table before you start working so hard?

LERITA: I am so conditioned to serve and care for men—that's what women and girls are socialized to do.

HH: Everybody needs some caring, gentleness, and tenderness. It's not a male need; it's a human need.

LERITA: I am always afraid that if I ask for some caring from a man, he'll leave.

HH: Then let him. Perhaps he needs to do some more healing so he can *give* rather than *take* in a relationship.

LERITA: Will it take forever to meet an enlightened man?

HH: Have a little faith.

LERITA: Faith?

HH: Lerita, if you must know, you are trying my patience with the endless questions.

LERITA: Is that something you are packing?

HH: Absolutely not. I hope your new heart brings lots of patience with it. Dealing with you sometimes takes all I have.

LERITA: But I want to make a point.

HH: What is it? What is the point?

LERITA: Is it as simple as having faith in God? I know lots of women who seem to have lots of faith, and they are struggling with men or struggling without men.

HH: "Faith without acts is dead." You've heard that famous Bible verse from the Book of James. People can't sit around passively waiting on some Higher Power. You must answer *your* calling and make healing a top priority. You have to act like you believe. You've got to sit down and *write* the book. God is not going to write it for you. Discipline is key. You cannot do anything without discipline. And, OK, maybe I forgot to mention listening to the little Voice.

LERITA: The little Voice? Didn't you bring that up before?

HH: Yes, see if you were having this talk with your stomach or intestines, you might have talked about following your gut. The little Voice is the same as following your gut or listening to the deepest part of the heart.

LERITA: Is it like intuition?

HH: Yes. Yes.

LERITA: OK, so what does the little Voice do?

HH: The little Voice guides you. It usually manifests as a feeling. You *feel* compelled or moved to call someone or do something. Coupled with faith, you can start to set healthy boundaries and express your disapproval about a man's behavior from a place of peace and strength. However, if I, your heart, is all clogged up with anger, resentment, anxiety, disappointment, and depression, it is very difficult to *hear* anything, let alone a quiet Voice.

LERITA: I understand the anger and resentment getting in the way, but how does carrying disappointment and depression in the heart block the little Voice?

HH: Being lighthearted, Lerita means just that. Think about it. Depression and disappointment are very heavy, thick feelings. They can pull you down so much that you are hardly aware of anything else. It's like being trapped in a dark cave. You cannot see the light outside nor hear the people on the surface trying to rescue you. The Voice is your rescue team calling to you, but the chatter in your mind is so full of doom and gloom that you cannot hear the help.

The other active negative emotions, like anger and anxiety, fill the mind with noisy chatter too. You can't hear the hushed Voice because a louder one is screaming in your head. Think about when you feel angry and anxious. You ruminate, repeating the same scene over and over in your head and reciting all of the things you thought you should have said. It's like a broken record.

LERITA: Are you saying that most people cannot hear the Voice?

HH: No. Personally, I feel the biggest problem is that many people hear the Voice but ignore it, aren't brave enough to follow it, or decide they know best. It's the same as lacking the courage to follow your heart when it comes to relationships. I am not talking about needy lust, where you are so desperate for attention and care that you ignore the obvious signs that someone is unsuitable for friendship or a romantic relationship. This is different. The Voice is your Guide, and it will get you through the worse of any kind of sexism or "dissing" as you describe it.

LERITA: I hope you're not packing up any courage.

HH: Oh no. I'm going to leave you with as much as possible. You are going to need it. Having a heart transplant will not be a piece of cake.

LERITA: You can say that again.

HH: Having a heart transplant...

LERITA: I didn't mean for you...

HH: (Laughing) Just a little heart humor. Have to keep you smiling. I may need to pack some of that seriousness of yours and whisper to your new heart to make having fun a top priority. You might get lucky and receive a heart from a young person who still knows how to play.

LERITA: Wait a minute. I know how to play.

HH: You could use some practice.

LERITA: Wow, look at the time! I need to run some errands. My "To Do list" is getting longer each day.

HH: Hmm, see what I mean. I'd better pack some of that time urgency too so you can hear the Voice better when it tells you to slow down and take a nap.

LERITA: You're right. I'm getting crazy. I need to talk more before I am placed on the UNOS Registry. I think I might have a few more things that I want you to pack in your suitcase.

HH: That's the spirit. That's my girl.

LERITA: Girl? Excuse me! I am a forty-...

HH: Lerita, "Please!" It was only a figure of speech. I meant it as a compliment. Please try to work on seeing *what is behind the words, behind the appearances,* what's really in someone's heart, OK?

LERITA: That sounds like another conversation. OK. I'll try.

Reflections

How do you respond to the "disruptions" in your life? Do you think your heart would interpret them differently?

What work or actions do you engage in with love in your heart?

Have you ever heard and followed the "still small Voice" or gut?

Can you compare what happened when you listened to your heart with when you did not listen?

A Garden of Jealousy and Envy

Since learning that I need a transplant, I have made it a point to talk to several transplant recipients. One lady from Michigan is enjoying her grandchildren for the first time. A gentleman is back to work full-time. Another guy is writing a book about his experiences. Talking to these survivors gives me hope. We discuss where the best transplant centers are and how protocols differ drastically from center to center. They all agree that the aftercare is the most vital part of the transplant process. They also insist that I must live close to a transplant facility during the first few months and be surrounded by loving, caring family members and friends.

It reminds me of how important my family is. They are why I choose to live. I am not ready to say goodbye to Mom, Dad, Kenneth, Robert, and Nicole. I come from a close family, and it makes such a difference. Regardless of our disagreements or holiday dramas, we are always there for each other. We always gather together for important occasions like graduations, weddings, and funerals. The importance of my career begins to dim as the transplant looms on the horizon.

On the other hand, life-threatening illnesses are often a test for intimate relationships, and sometimes spouses and children cannot handle the trauma and stress. One recipient spoke of his wife having a gathering of her friends at the house when he arrived home from the hospital. For him, it was the beginning of the end of their marriage. I'm not sure if being single is detrimental. Certainly, I wouldn't want any more drama in the middle of a heart transplant, yet it would be nice to have someone devoted to my recovery telling me, "Baby, it's going to be all right." I know another body is not the answer. I need a very special person, one who is willing to join me on this roller coaster ride.

Despite my lack of control over this impending event, I want to feel like I have some say in what happens to me. I put together a living will and appoint some advocates. With a living will, I can specify if I want to be resuscitated and how long I want to remain on life support. I select 40 days and 40 nights if I take a turn for the worse. Since I know my parents will not be able emotionally to monitor the doctors, I give my friends Gail, Rebecca and Martha the authority to make decisions for me if I am unconscious. I also give Gail power of attorney over the transplant medication fund she established for me. Now I am closer to being mentally and physically prepared to give up my heart.

LERITA: Good afternoon.

HH: Oh hi.

LERITA: Have you been trying to contact me?

HH: No, I've been pretty busy with the packing and all.

LERITA: You sound so happy about it.

HH: Yes, I feel excited about the trip. I haven't done anything like this before—well at least not alone. But I am more excited for you.

LERITA: Yeah, right. I guess one of us should be happy.

HH: I don't understand you, Lerita, really I don't. How could you *not* be happy?

LERITA: I *am* happy in there somewhere. Right now, it is clouded with sadness. You, my closest friend and companion for the past 40 something years, are leaving. Don't you get it? You're leaving—*forever*.

HH: Yes, but it is for a good cause. You'll be happier and healthier.

LERITA: I know the sadness will pass and one day I'll think about you and smile. But right now it hurts.

HH: Here, let me give you a big hug. Is that better?

LERITA: Is that where the term "warm-hearted" comes from? Is it my heart giving me a hug?

HH: You didn't know that?

LERITA: Not really. It makes sense, though. What are you packing now?

HH: Dear, that resentment stuff—*from 40 years*—was too large for the bag I had. I had to look for a trunk. You didn't spill all of the beans. You have a lot of contempt for men, most politicians, many of your colleagues, rich people, hospitals, especially doctors. I could go on. You and I have been carrying a heavy load. I am sure you have more. What's next?

LERITA: How about some jealousy and envy?

HH: Haven't we touched on that before?

LERITA: Yes, we *touched* on it, but I think hauling some of it out of my heart is going to take more than a touch.

HH: If it was anything like the resentment...

LERITA: Don't get carried away. You talked to me about getting upset when I hear about the accomplishments of others. It's true; it's hard for me to watch television or hear the radio without thinking, "I should be doing that." I understand that I cannot do everything. You've helped me to see that I, like everyone else, have special talents. Yet I cannot seem to connect it all. Rather than focusing on cultivating the gift, whatever it may be, I seem to be immobilized by feelings of jealousy and envy. I feel like I am falling behind.

HH: Still in the race, huh? No wonder we're so tired all of the time. Look at all of that mental energy you are wasting. Now I know you've heard this analogy a thousand times, but you like to garden, right?

LERITA: Yes, I love beautiful flowers and vegetables. but...

HH: OK. You've seen some beautiful gardens, large and small, correct?

LERITA: Definitely.

HH: Can you imagine wanting a garden so badly that you spend the majority of your time standing around in other people's gardens wishing yours looked like that? When would you have time to plant and cultivate your own?

LERITA: That sounds too simple.

HH: Life is not that complex Lerita, but you seem to take pride in making it complicated. It is important to check out the magnificent gardens and to talk with the gardeners. All of the information will help you with yours. But you cannot grow a doggone thing if you are not putting in some hard work. You can turn to other people for guidance. Then you must get outside, plant, fertilize, check for bugs, and pray for rain and sun. Gardens, like gifts and talents, need cultivation, and that takes time and attention.

LERITA: Plants and flowers are so amazing. They keep coming back after those harsh winters with snow, and ice—things that you would think would kill them forever.

HH: That's true. You, too, are like a flower responding to the seasons of life. There is a time to plant new seeds and a time for shoots to rise up through the soil. Do you know how powerful new growth is? It can blast through rock. Then there is the harvest of summer—the results of all of that hard work. There's fall when it's time to let go, get rid of stuff in preparation for the cold winter ahead. Finally, there's winter; a time to let roots deepen in the soil, and hibernate. Each season is wonderful, but the tasks are different.

LERITA: What a nice way to describe it, the seasons of life.

HH: Remember, Lerita, there are also different kinds of flowers and plants. There are hot summer vegetables like tomatoes and peppers and cold winter crops like collard greens and cabbage. Perennials come back each year; annuals aren't quite so hardy. Bulbs are different. They actually need a harsh, cold winter. People are like that too. Some are perennials; others aren't quite so hardy. Yet others need challenging lives in order to bloom later. Being jealous and envious of others only uses up energy that you could use in nurturing your own talents. Hard work, sometimes known as *practice,* is essential. Like I said before, developing your natural talents requires work—and *trying* is not *doing.* Doing is doing. Wishing for a glorious garden is nice, but it won't produce a beautiful one.

LERITA: This is some quick counsel.

HH: It doesn't have to take all day. Listen. Let me know if I'm going to need another trunk for the jealousy and envy. Knowing you, I suspect there will be some left over even after I take the bulk of it. Your new heart will have to work with you to make regular dumps. Weekly pickups are so much better than letting the trash pile up.

LERITA: (Laughing) So true. Thanks. I'll let you go now.

HH: OK. Talk with you tomorrow.

Reflections

Have you ever wished that you were someone else or living someone else's life? What are your own unique gifts and talents, and how can you cultivate them?

Do you have any jealousy and envy that you could turn into constructive actions?

What "work" (similar to the work of gardening like watering, weeding, and pruning) could you do to promote more peace and joy in your life?

Shame, Shame, Shame

I've led a lonely life for many months. Avoidance is my modus operandi. I don't want people to know how awful I feel. I struggle to walk and must stop to rest when I become short of breath. Often I try to will my body further but my legs, in particular, refuse. I frequent restrooms more to rest than to use the toilet. Relative to other heart failure patients, I maneuver quite well. Yet my stamina diminishes each day. I can barely keep it together. Since fatigue is my frequent companion, when I arrive home from work exhausted, I toss a coin to determine if I eat or sleep first. Sleep usually wins.

I feel so tired, tired of my body, tired of my life, tired of being tired. Some days I think I feel the fatigue of every other heart failure patient in the world. I know their physical and mental weariness. I wonder if I can maintain until the transplant. I look at the three flights of stairs to my office and then slowly walk over to the elevator. I want to finish the academic year, but the schedule of lecturing, research, office hours, and a host of other professional activities is wearing me down. I struggled with fatigue during the gorgeous days of Indian summer, and now that the cold Colorado winter draws near, I find it virtually impossible to navigate the freezing cold with a failing heart.

I do not want anything to jeopardize the transplant, especially since it has been approved. I choose not to share these heart conversations with my team of doctors. I worry that they will think the idea is bizarre and that I am crazy. I've only shown them to a few close friends. I don't think people would understand how the heart talks sustain me. The conversations are my best coping mechanism. Aside from the physical trauma, I suffer from anticipatory grief. I am going to lose my heart. I sob daily. My heart is dying so I may live. Someone will die so I may live. I am so sad.

LERITA: Hi there.

HH: My, aren't we chummy today.

LERITA: Oh you don't like my greeting?

HH: Oh it's fine. I was listening more to your tone of voice. You know you sound very different than you did the first time we talked.

LERITA: I was very angry then.

HH: I know. Sounds like you forgave me.

LERITA: I am getting there. I guess I see things differently; see you differently.

HH: Oh yeah?

LERITA: Yes. It isn't your fault that you arrived diseased and will have to leave. You've performed way beyond the call of duty and under some pretty stressful circumstances. You've never stopped on me. I haven't fainted on the street, or been rushed to the emergency room. The wisdom you've tried to communicate to me over the years, and especially in the last few months, is immeasurable. What more can I ask for?

HH: Probably a heart that could stay with you until the end.

LERITA: Don't say it like that. I suppose we both would have liked being together longer. It's like discovering a lost love. I cannot believe that I finally start to really talk with you and establish an intimate relationship, and then you have to leave.

HH: You'll be able to talk with your new heart.

LERITA: But I won't know it like I do you, and it won't know me. We'll have to start over.

HH: Sometimes a new start is good. But what you say is true. It will take some time for the two of you to feel comfortable, like any good relationship. You have to take time to get to know each other.

LERITA: I worry what my new heart will be like. Will it possess your personality? Your sense of humor? What if we get into a fight like you and I did during the first conversation?

HH: I see you are leaning toward the pessimistic side today. I think they work on trying to make good matches.

LERITA: DNA wise, yes, I suppose, but I didn't call you to talk about that anyway.

HH: I know.

LERITA: You're being a smart-ass again.

HH: Living inside of you, it only comes naturally.

LERITA: That was low.

HH: Sorry but it is so tempting to play around with you, Lerita. You set yourself up all of the time. Besides, you know I am not mean-spirited or should I say, "hard hearted."

LERITA: Had to get in a heart pun, huh?

HH: Of course I did. Now, what's on your mind?

LERITA: I found something else I think you should pack.

HH: Are we going to need a truck?

LERITA: There you go again.

HH: (Chuckling) Can't you take a joke? Actually, I think it is good you are clearing out your heart-space. Things won't be so "heavy" for your new heart.

LERITA: His or her name won't be Heavy Harvey?

HH: Definitely not. I am one of a kind.

LERITA: You're too much. I guess there's a certain joy attached to being light-hearted. When I think of letting go of resentment, anger, jealousy and envy, I can imagine how much lighter I'll feel.

HH: Yes, and it's even better: You begin with a clear heart space. What else would you like me to take?

LERITA: How about some shame, feelings of inadequacy and insecurity?

HH: Sounds like a tall order. Are there any things in particular that you feel ashamed or inadequate about? Wait. Let me guess. It's something to do with your professional life and something to do with your personal life?

LERITA: Ha, ha. That takes care of it, huh?

HH: I swear I've never seen anything like it. You have let others get to you, Lerita. You've let others define too much of who you think you are.

LERITA: Aren't we getting ahead of ourselves? I haven't had a chance to explain yet.

HH: Oh sorry. I was jumping to conclusions. What are some of the things you feel ashamed about? I mean how could you feel inadequate given all that you've accomplished in a scant 40 years?

LERITA: Oh, there are the usual things I suppose. You know how kids talk about each other. Early on, I felt ashamed because I was skinny. Julia, my Creole girlfriend during elementary school, made a big deal out of hair—mine was "nappy" and needed pressing, hers was naturally straight. Later on, when I was a teenager, my brother talked about how unattractive I was and that I would never get a boyfriend. My lack of success at happy relationships in high school seemed to confirm his prediction.

HH: Was it the way other people made you feel or how you felt inside? By the way, do you know of any teenagers who are in happy relationships?

LERITA: I know. I know. I suspect there have always been people—girlfriends, brothers, family—who felt threatened by my precocity. I was smart, quick, and I worked extra hard. I think it made some of them feel inadequate.

HH: Did you do it on purpose?

LERITA: Do what on purpose?

HH: Try to make them feel inadequate by showing what a know-it-all you were?

LERITA: Well, sometimes.

HH: Uh huh. So you kept the cycle going.

LERITA: They tried to beat me down to keep me in my place. Dad didn't want me to become conceited, "get too big for my britches," he said, so he rarely if ever complimented me. Kenneth, my brother, was jealous of the attention I received because I was a good student and a dutiful daughter. In fact, sometimes I think he detested me because he thought I tried to appear perfect, a model child. He once said I acted nice because all I wanted was attention.

HH: There's some truth there. You've always needed lots of attention, Lerita.

LERITA: I don't now.

HH: Hallelujah for that. We won't go into the crazy things you've engaged in because you needed attention. It's a miracle that we are still alive.

LERITA: It's not been that bad.

HH: Do you remember the time...?

LERITA: Never mind. You don't have to remind me.

HH: Lerita, all of that childhood and growing up stuff is understandable, but are you telling me that you still carry a load of shame and insecurity?

LERITA: Yes. I think the shame comes and goes, but I fear the judgments of others.

HH: You let what you perceive others *might* be thinking, determine what you do or say?

LERITA: Is that so uncommon? Yes, I imagine what others might think when I dress for the day or if I decide to participate in some activities.

HH: That's sad, Lerita. Perhaps you need to take a different stance. What if you considered why you're involved in the first place?

LERITA: What do you mean?

HH: I think you need to ask yourself constantly, "What is the purpose—what is this for?"

LERITA: Go on.

HH: Well Lerita, I am sorry to use this expression: You achieve a lot of goals, but your heart's not in it.

LERITA: Oh no not that heart pun...

HH: It works here. Look at all of the activities that you are a part of—committees at work, advising students, counseling family and friends day and night, then there is church and all of your commitments there. You don't do all of these things because you have a passion or a love for them, but because you are *driven* by this insecurity, this deficiency you speak of. Unfortunately, that kind of life pushes the joy way down in your heart, and you never get a chance to feel it.

LERITA: I have done everything because I am driven?

HH: Name me something that you've pursued just for fun, for the joy of it.

LERITA: I like learning. I went to grad school because I found the study of psychology intellectually intriguing and...

HH: Lerita? You went to Harvard. You picked all elite institutions for graduate school.

LERITA: I wanted the best graduate training.

HH: Look you are talking to me, your heart. Let's tell the whole truth here. You needed to prove that you were smart but I'm not sure to whom. We knew that already. You entered this life with intelligence. And you would have been a lot happier if you had taken a year off and later pursued counseling psychology, which they didn't offer at Harvard. But you were scared that if you stopped, you wouldn't go back, and you definitely were afraid to pass up Harvard. So you took off on a detour, and you haven't found your way back. When I'm gone, please remember to ask, "What's the purpose; what is this for?" before pursuing anything.

LERITA: Why? Why is that so important?

HH: Then you'll know when you are living from your spirit instead of being *driven* by feelings of shame or inadequacy or your need to please or get approval, basically your ego stuff. It's been hard for you to tell the difference, but you'll never get out of the ego trap otherwise.

LERITA: I don't know how to do that.

HH: Sure you do. Just keep asking the questions: "What is the purpose?" "Why am I doing this?" "Am I doing this to please someone, to make certain they like me or is it something I feel drawn to or compelled to do from the inside?"

LERITA: What if people get mad when I refuse a request? I hate to disappoint them.

HH: If they are your true friends, they'll get over it. The question, though, is always how do *you* feel? Do you feel at peace? Is there some joy welling up inside? Really Lerita, it's the only way out of the torment you're in.

LERITA: Sometimes I think I'll never be able to move beyond the hell.

HH: Healing takes time. It rarely happens in an instant. Besides, that is what you are here on earth for, Lerita. Healing. But as you know, healing can be painful.

LERITA: Why?

HH: You might not get the lesson otherwise.

LERITA: So what?

HH: Then you might need to repeat it. Trials and tribulations are lessons you didn't get the first time. They keep coming back until you do.

LERITA: Please no repeats.

HH: Yes, but for some hard-headed people, present company excluded of course, it may take a few times. It's OK. Goodness, you are certainly going to need to remember these tips when you have the transplant.

LERITA: Did you have to bring that up? We were having such a pleasant conversation. OK, what kind of lesson am I getting with this trauma? I already had open-heart surgery.

HH: You're right. Since you didn't get it the first time, you're sure to get it this time. Don't you understand what all of this means, Lerita? You must make a *change in heart*—the physical one and the emotional one. Here's your opportunity to clean the slate; start over and fill your heart with things that will make it sing, that will make us happy. Not everyone gets a chance to make a change in heart. Lots of people die with heavy hearts filled with anger, disappointment, anxiety and hate.

LERITA: So the transplant is about getting some of this stuff out of my heart?

HH: Symbolically, yes. Like I said, a *change in heart*. It's a change of what's in your heart and how you live your life as a result.

LERITA: Including the shame and inadequacy?

HH: Yes, the shame and inadequacy are clogging it up.

LERITA: I guess I have been comparing myself to the guys in my department.

HH: … Whose lives are very different. Why compare yourself to your male colleagues, many of whom are doing little else with their lives besides building their resumes? Furthermore, you never apply the litmus test.

LERITA: The litmus test?

HH: A quick and simple one. Are they happy? Do they exude peace and joy, or are they more driven than you? When you see them, do you want to be around them or do you want to run away from their anxiety, tension or depression? How many of those stars in your department are truly shining and enjoying life?

LERITA: I don't know. I mean, are we supposed to enjoy life? If so, I don't know many people who meet that criteria.

HH: For as long as you and I can remember, you've been tense or anxious about something. What have you enjoyed? Going to school? Having a big time job...?

LERITA: I enjoy spending time with my friends, although sometimes I worry about whether they like me.

HH: You were right when you said you had a lot of insecurity to unload. Wouldn't it be nice not to have to be concerned about whether people like you or not?

LERITA: That's hard to do.

HH: Time to wake up, Lerita. Boy, we have a lot of work to do, and there isn't much time.

LERITA: We've got at least six to eight weeks. The doctors say if I go on the list soon, the transplant might happen that quickly since I live out here in Colorado, "the wild west." There are not many transplant centers nearby competing for the same organs.

HH: (Mumbling) That's what you think.

LERITA: What did you say?

HH: Oh nothing. That you must shrink the list of things blocking the joy in your heart. Then you must change what *you* think about yourself—it cannot be determined by what others perceive. Remember this please, Lerita: *If you learn about yourself from the inside, no one can ever define you from the outside.*

LERITA: Now that is something to ponder, Heavy. No wonder I feel so insecure and inadequate. I've been letting others define me. I will definitely take some time to reflect on who I am without all of the Greek chorus commentary.

HH: Yes! Look, I understand the loneliness that you experience sometimes, Lerita, and how do we get over it?

LERITA and HH: (In unison) Start by doing things that make my heart sing!

HH: Hey, I see you have absorbed some of my previous counsel.

LERITA: Actually, I've started cultivating a relationship with myself. I tend to some of my own needs. It's not that I don't allow others to take care of me, but I don't sit around waiting for people. I share the things I like with friends, like going to movies, reading or going out for dinner. But I enjoy those things on my own too.

HH: Are you happy?

LERITA: I could be better. A little companionship wouldn't hurt, but I know I can get that from a variety of sources. It doesn't have to be a romantic relationship, but being in one would be nice. I am happy that I don't feel ashamed anymore about not having a husband. It is OK to be single.

HH: I'm grateful that you've made some peace about that.

LERITA: I still want to find out more about who am I, the real me from the inside. How do I do that?

HH: By listening to the silence.

LERITA: Listening to the silence?

HH: We've covered this territory before, but some lessons are worth repeating. Just remember that "listen" and "silent" contain exactly the same letters. Listen within to learn who you truly are and what you are guided to do. But you have to be silent to hear. Try cutting out some of that outside noise and inside chatter.

LERITA: Listen and silent. Same letters. Wow. That sounds easy enough.

HH: It isn't. Have you noticed how many crazy thoughts twirl around in your mind? And you are not a good listener. You are always interrupting people. Instead of listening to them you're working on your comeback. Listening is a skill worth developing.

LERITA: I've been listening to you.

HH: It took 40 years and a heart...

LERITA: Don't start.

HH: Look, I gotta go. I think I am going to need to arrange for something larger to pack up this stuff. Is there anything else?

LERITA: Oh I'm sure there are some little things. I could be more organized, more focused...

HH: I think all of those items are tied to the heavies we've talked about already. I suspect if we can remove some of the shame and feelings of inadequacy out of your heart, those minor issues will take care of themselves. They've nearly driven you insane.

LERITA: Insane? I think that's pushing it.

HH: Fair. But where's the peace and joy in your life, Lerita? OK, that's another conversation. We can talk about that later.

LERITA: All right. Thanks.

HH: For what?

LERITA: For helping me to see what's clogging up my heart.

HH: Couldn't point it out without your willingness. It takes courage and often it is very painful to look inside your heart. Your new heart will be grateful that you took some time to clear some space. It will make the transition easier.

LERITA: OK.

HH: Until next time.

Reflections

Do you need to unload some feelings of shame and inadequacy from your heart? What can you replace them with?

Are you often concerned about what others think of you? Do you know why that matters to you?

Are there things you are doing that you're not sure why you're doing them?

A Heart Full of Disappointment

I have always thought of myself as a deeply spiritual person, but my apprehension about the heart transplant is telling. I'm starting to question what spirituality means to me. Do I feel that the Spirit of God is in everybody and everything, and I should act accordingly? Do I believe that the Spirit guides me at every turn on this winding road of life? What exactly *am* I hearing, if anything, when I sit in silence?

A few years ago, I began seeking inner guidance for every major decision, including choices about houses and jobs. Sometimes I seek guidance about trips and dating, although I notice that I don't always follow the wisdom I receive. What's so uncanny about this practice, as Heavy Harvey points out, is that the guidance typically emerges from silence. It occurs during a quiet time in the morning, or as I slowly awaken from a nap, on a silent retreat or outside in the stillness. Now, as I face this life-threatening event, I need more frequent and intimate contact with some greater wisdom. I need to know whether or not it's God who wants me to have this transplant because I certainly don't. The thought of changing my life in such a drastic way is unfathomable.

During my last hospital visit in late November, Dr. Bloomberg stopped by my bed to chat with me. "Are you ready for the transplant?" she asked. "Am I ready?" "Am I ready?" "Am I ready?" reverberated through my head. I know I remain unprepared. I am not psychologically prepared, I am not emotionally prepared, and, above all, I am not spiritually prepared. Do I have enough trust in God to go through with this? Dr. Bloomberg and I both know I am in trouble. The second bout of heart failure, in less than two weeks, is serious, and we've both seen my latest echocardiograms. I am running out of time. "Are you ready to go on the national organ transplant waiting list?" she queried. I know that once I am listed, I can be called at any time, even tomorrow.

The weekend in the hospital is a real eye-opener. To my astonishment, my roommate and I have some things in common. We are both 41 years old, very ill, African-American women. Angela, however, has five children whose ages range from 4 to 24. She is suffering from moyamoya disease, a medical condition that results in mini-strokes. She lost the use of her right arm, and she needs speech therapy. Periodically she sneaks outside to smoke. As I watch her children march back and forth across the room calling out, "Mama," I reflect on my own life. I could have been her. I could have chosen to marry, have five children, and get divorced. Yet I cannot imagine being this ill with five dependent children. Compared to Angela, I have no reason to be dissatisfied. So why *am* I experiencing so much disappointment about my life?

My mind wanders back to being denied tenure at the University of Michigan and my crazy dream to win the Nobel Prize in psychology that doesn't exist. I constantly chastise myself about not achieving more in my field of social psychology. Where is my American Psychological Association Early Career Award or my MacArthur Genius Grant or Guggenheim Fellowship? My obsessional thinking focuses on my status as a single woman and correcting the perceived flaws that prevent me from finding a husband. I know my family and friends wonder if I'll ever step into a wedding gown and walk down the aisle. Now I am faced with a heart transplant! Can it get any worse?

It is time for me to make a decision about being listed with UNOS. Though inconceivable by my own rational standards, I become consumed with thoughts of work. I decide it is not the end of the semester, and I cannot leave my classes, my students, and my research before finals. Who would finish teaching my courses, give and grade my exams, and calculate final grades? It is too overwhelming, even for my workaholic personality. So I tell Dr. Bloomberg that I am waiting on a "sign," some inner guidance about the transplant. She looks at me incredulously, perhaps thinking "this visit to the hospital is not a sign?" Graciously, she says, "Well, let us know when you are ready," and walks out of the room. I turn to Heavy, hoping he can help me know what I should do. I reason that it is now the first week of November and I have only four more weeks of classes. Yet I feel nothing besides fatigue and exhaustion. I wonder if I will survive until the transplant.

LERITA: Hey, heart.

HH: Is that any way to get my attention?

LERITA: I could have said, "What's up, heart?"

HH: Neither one seems appropriate.

LERITA: But it got your attention, didn't it?

HH: I guess so. What do you want?

LERITA: What's wrong with you? You sound awfully moody today.

HH: You too. I guess I am in a funk today.

LERITA: You're in a funk? About what?

HH: Lerita, you're not the only one who is sad about my leaving. I have feelings too. I am going to miss you. I am going to miss pumping and trying to convey some direction and guidance.

LERITA: You're actually going to miss me?

HH: I will miss these heart-to-heart talks. It's hard to leave a nearly 42-year-old relationship. I wish I could stay to see how the rest of your life turns out. But I know, in order for you to flourish, I've got to give up the ghost.

LERITA: Please don't say it like that.

HH: It's been done before, and I'm not the only one. Someone may be dying right now, and you will live because their family will be kind enough to donate his or her heart.

LERITA: Right now? Someone is dying?

HH: They may not know it yet, but, yes, they are preparing to die. Hopefully, you'll remember that and cherish the gift of life. There are so many wonderful things for you to do, Lerita. After the transplant, I'm sure you won't waste a moment of time. Enjoy your family and friends because you will be living on "borrowed time," shall I say?

LERITA: Did you have to remind me? Sounds like a lot of pressure.

HH: Don't make it stressful. Think about what you would do if you only had six months to live. I hope you won't spend it working.

LERITA: I am deeply concerned about my job and how long I am going to be away from it.

HH: That's precisely it. Think about the transplant as an opportunity to redesign your life, for it to be happier, more peaceful and joyful. Hopefully, you can put aside some of your professional anxiety and the striving to be extraordinary. Wouldn't it be nice if you could wake up each day and feel contented?

LERITA: I'd give anything for that.

HH: The transplant recovery will help.

LERITA: It will?

HH: You'll be a different person. It will take a year or more.

LERITA: A year? But they said...

HH: I know of what I speak, Lerita. Unfortunately, your recovery will take much longer than three months. That's mainly because you are very bull-headed. You always have to learn things the hard way.

LERITA: I don't know about that, I...

HH: Listen, I know. That's why I am so tired. But you contacted me tonight to talk about something else.

LERITA: Yes, I forgot about one more thing that I want you to pack up and take with you.

HH: More stuff? Actually, I am glad. You'll have extra room for your new heart to sing and dance. What is it?

LERITA: I feel very disappointed.

HH: You're right about that. It is so heavy and thick it has almost suffocated me at times. I was wondering when you were going to mention it. I thought disappointments would be at the top of the list.

LERITA: You did?

HH: Yes, you have enough disappointment to fill a van.

LERITA: Is it that bad?

HH: Why do you think my name is Heavy Harvey? Why do you think our disease worsened to the point that they can't fix it? Why do you think my muscles have thickened to the point that I can hardly pump?

LERITA: You attribute all of that to my being disappointed with life?

HH: I am heavy with your disappointments and resentments, your jealousy and envy, shame and feelings of inadequacy, your contempt, and...

LERITA: OK. OK. I get the picture.

HH: The disappointment, though, is the heaviest of all. And remember, you named it first a couple of months ago when you listed the things in your heart. There's more disappointment than anything.

LERITA: Sort of like the label on food products that provide the list of ingredients?

HH: Right. So the first one listed is the item the product contains most of. Why didn't you work on disappointment first?

LERITA: It didn't occur to me immediately. I was caught off guard during that first conversation about packing. As I reflected on these conversations, I realized that I need you to take the disappointment. I don't know why I have so much. I guess I hate living in this hellhole of a world. What is there to look forward to? Nothing has turned out like I thought it would.

HH: I can tell you why you have so much disappointment.

LERITA: I bet you can. Let's hear it.

HH: You've been set up.

LERITA: Set up? By whom?

HH: By the world.

LERITA: Come again?

HH: Disappointment is the difference between your expectations and what happened.

LERITA: OK. So what?

HH: Haven't we talked about your expectations?

LERITA: I guess so.

HH: I'll ask you this. What *did* you expect to happen in your life?

LERITA: If we go back to, let's say, when I graduated from high school, I'd say I expected to go to college, meet Prince Charming, get married, have a couple of kids, earn a master's degree, become a high school guidance counselor and live happily ever after.

HH: Happily ever after? Right. We'll come back to that. Anything else?

LERITA: Oh, I dunno, a nice house, nice neighborhood, some fun family activities, and vacations. Sound pretty dull?

HH: Sounds like the typical American dream. So what happened?

LERITA: You know what happened. I met someone that I thought was Prince Charming in college, but I changed. I discovered an intellectual side, and I decided I wanted to become a college professor. I needed a Ph.D., but Charles, my boyfriend, said he wouldn't transfer his job from San Francisco to Boston. I went without him.

HH: "Change." Remember that word.

LERITA: All right. Then I earned my Ph.D. and started teaching at Michigan. I wanted to get tenure and make a big splash in psychology.

HH: Yes, I remember, and you also wanted to win that Nobel Prize that they don't give in psychology.

LERITA: Did you have to bring that up?

HH: Let's put all of the cards on the table here, Lerita.

LERITA: Then I was denied tenure. Talk about a disappointment.

HH: Devastation is a better description. You almost killed us over that incident.

LERITA: Do you have to mention that too?

HH: Honesty is the best policy when dealing with matters of the heart.

LERITA: Couldn't get through one of these conversations without a heart pun, could you?

HH: It wouldn't be a real heart-to-heart talk between us without one or two.

LERITA: (Laughing) You're pitiful.

HH: Because I have a sense of humor? Come now. But back to your story.

LERITA: I was denied tenure, so I moved to Tennessee even though I didn't want to. I bought a beautiful home, but still no husband.

HH: Really expected to have that man?

LERITA: Doesn't every woman?

HH: Go on.

LERITA: Three years later, I ended up at the University of Colorado, and I love it here. But here I am, in my 40s, no husband, no children, and having a heart transplant. What do I have to look forward to except more loneliness and illness?

HH: Who told you that you must find a man and get married?

LERITA: I don't know. Didn't we cover that in the last conversation?

HH: Did you stop to think what would have been best for you?

LERITA: What do you mean?

HH: Your purpose in life is different, Lerita. Your path might not include the "typical" journey with a husband and children.

LERITA: Possibly. Sometimes I look at other people with their children and think there are some things I could miss.

HH: And why must you make a splash in psychology?

LERITA: Because that is what is expected in my field.

HH: *Expected?* Really, everybody has to be a star? How can anyone be an outstanding researcher, teacher, spouse, parent, and contributor to the community? Something has to suffer.

LERITA: Yeah, and from what I've observed with my colleagues and friends, it is usually the children. You mean no one can have it all?

HH: Don't you see, Lerita? You've tried to live according to worldly expectations. Yet you and no one else here is *of this world*. You're a spiritual being in a human body, and this world is not your home. So, when you try to follow the path of the world, it leads to nowhere.

LERITA: You're getting deep on me again, Heavy. Path leading to nowhere?

HH: Ah, I should correct myself. It leads to disappointment and dissatisfaction. In the world, you can never do enough. You can be a shining star one day and not even in the sky the next, that is, according to the standards of the world.

LERITA: You have a point. I think many people are trying to have their 15 minutes of fame and to prolong it.

HH: Then there is the issue of *change*. Things always change in the world. Economic conditions change. Physical environments change. Political times change. Emotions change. Perceptions change. People change. You change. People age. Children grow up. People get ill. You got ill. People die.

LERITA: I am ill. Am I going to die?

HH: One day you will release this body. But you won't die from having a heart transplant, Lerita. That is the whole point. You made that choice already—between dying and living with a transplant.

LERITA: Changes. Why do things always have to change?

HH: You don't like change even when it is good.

LERITA: Change is scary. I like the familiar.

HH: Even when it hurts and holds you back?

LERITA: I guess so.

HH: Sounds like a life sentence to me. Change is inevitable. You know that.

LERITA: Can we talk about something else?

HH: Is the conversation getting too challenging for you? Too close to that fear you've been carrying around in your heart?

LERITA: You know about that too?

HH: Of course. You're afraid to let go of the past, afraid to open yourself up to a new life. You've gotten so comfortable with pain, disappointment, anxiety, and a schedule that is out-of-control that you cannot imagine another way. Your fear is not of dying, but of living—living the kind of life that you want instead of settling for the kind of life you have. You're frightened, all right, but not about what you think.

LERITA: I don't know how to be any different.

HH: Lerita, you can't lead anyone else's life. That's why it is important to follow the urgings of your heart. They come from within your soul. They reflect your true nature, not the self that you have constructed to adapt to the world. As long as you try to fulfill all of the expectations you've internalized that are projected on you by others, you'll always be a prisoner, a slave. You'll be unhappy and disillusioned because they don't reflect who you really are. They're societal or family expectations.

LERITA: I feel like I've been running in place for several years, and you're right, I am not happy. I remember thinking last summer when I returned to Colorado after being on vacation that I was sick of my life. I felt joyless.

HH: That's when we had that major heart failure incident that got us to the transplant workup. Don't you see the connection?

LERITA: Yes. I was sick of my life, so I decided it was time to check out.

HH: My prayers were answered, thank God.

LERITA: With a transplant?

HH: Yes, Lerita. You need this *change in heart.* Look, I have to go. I'd better arrange for some additional moving equipment.

LERITA: Need that moving van, huh?

HH: I didn't want to offend you but...

LERITA: (Laughing) I know I have a lot of issues.

HH: Lerita, you are not alone. Everyone who comes into this world has healing to do. Yours will be more public as a way to show others what they need to do to heal their lives. Most people have two and three van loads of stuff that they need to release from their hearts or remove from their kidneys or livers, to use the organ analogies. If people would pay attention to what is happening in their lives; if they would stop and take a moment to look past the physical aspects of their illnesses, similar to what you're doing, healing could begin. You're not the only one with heart trouble. Everyone has things to clean up and clear out of their hearts.

LERITA: Heart trouble—another pun?

HH: Not really. But it would make a good one don't you think?

LERITA: I guess so, but it's not one of your best. How do I stop thinking like this? What about others who have troubled hearts? Not everyone can have a transplant. Not everyone needs or would want a transplant.

HH: You're right about that. Clearing out the negative emotions in the heart is absolutely essential. A change in heart is a transformation in how you *feel* about yourself, about your family, about your friends, about your life. It doesn't matter if you smile and say kind words. It doesn't matter what kind of car you drive, or how many houses you own. Your heart always holds your true feelings. Remember it's what's in your heart that counts.

LERITA: That's a wonderful idea, but you didn't answer my question.

HH: I do get carried away sometimes don't I?

LERITA: Yes, you do.

HH: I am *your* heart. Have you forgotten? Look, let's talk again later. I promise I'll answer your question but let's save it for another conversation. I think we both need some rest.

LERITA: OK, but you promise?

HH: I promise. So long for now.

LERITA: Cheers.

Reflections

Do you feel sometimes that you are living someone else's vision for your life, one conveyed to you through their expectations?

Do you feel that your heart is heavy with emotions like anger, resentment, feelings of inadequacy or disappointment? If so, how might you find ways to release these emotions that burden the heart?

How would you redesign your life?

Letting Go of My Heart: The Final Goodbye

I shop for and wrap Christmas gifts. I grade final papers. My physicians marvel at my energy level since I move in and out of heart failure regularly and my ejection fraction (how powerfully my heart beats) remains quite low. How I am able to roll out of bed, dress myself and drive to my office mystifies even me.

The holidays are wonderful with my family as we gather at Kenneth's home in Oakland. Despite whatever discord occurred in the past, it is very important for me to hug, kiss and express my love to Mom, Dad, Kenneth, Robert, and Nicole. We share delicious meals. We laugh, and we cry, not knowing if this is the last time we will all be together as a family. Facing death in this way allows me to see each person in a different light. As I celebrate, I have no idea when I will say farewell to Heavy Harvey. I cannot imagine our final conversation.

I feel very edgy on the flight back to Denver. Unbeknownst to me, I had experienced heart failure on previous flights. Airlines set the cabin pressure at about 7,000 feet and being at a higher altitude causes fluid to back up in my lungs because my poor weak heart cannot pump hard enough. I pray that my heart will hold up for the flight home.

It is now Sunday evening, January 8, 1995. I scurry around trying to complete a dozen or more things on the "to do" list. Carrying around the beeper since last Thursday serves as a constant reminder that I could be called at any time. After talking to my dear friend, Gail, we both agree that I should remain calm and act as if I will be "beeped" sometime in February, around Valentine's Day. Yes, February would be an excellent time to receive a new heart. I will have approximately a month to organize my life so I can embark on this unimaginable adventure.

I fall into bed surrounded by a mound of pillows usually reserved for propping up my swollen feet and my head to avoid shortness of breath. Lately, due to the increasingly frequent bouts of heart failure, the spacious queen-size bed feels like a surrogate lover, pillows kissing my tears, sheets and blankets hugging me through my days of terror and trepidation. Tonight I am dog-tired, the constant fatigue growing more each day. I lie there momentarily thinking about the few tasks I want to accomplish tomorrow. I need temporary plates for the car I just purchased, and I have to pay the bills that are due. Then there is my teaching schedule—who is going to substitute for me and when. I cannot believe I am the protagonist in this tale. Here I am, a 41-year-old, single, African-American female psychology professor having a heart transplant at the beginning of the semester. How can this be happening?

Because I am so exhausted, I turn off the ringer on the phone. I know I am wrong, but I do not want to be awakened. I need the rest and each time the phone rings, I jump. Margaret Waller, the transplant coordinator, warned me that they would contact me about a donor heart by phoning first and then activate the beeper, if I didn't answer. I hear a little whisper, a quiet urging by my dear, sweet failing heart, asking me where the beeper is. Where *is* the beeper I wonder? I remember that at some point, I hooked it to my purse, but where is my purse? I think, "There is no way I want to get out of bed." But the inner Voice returns, louder this time, chanting, "Where is the beeper? Where is the beeper?" Reluctantly, I slowly rise, walk downstairs and look for my purse. I find it on the kitchen floor with the beeper attached. Plodding up the stairs to my room, I drag my purse behind me and throw it on the rug next to the bed. Okay. Now I can get some sleep. I eye the clock, and it is about 10:45 p.m. In no time, I am "dead to the world" as I describe my bone-tired sleep.

Suddenly I awake because I think I hear the beeper. I peer at the clock in the darkness and make out the time: 12:17 a.m. I sit up in bed and reach for the light. I look down at my purse. "Another dream about the beeper going off," I mumble. The recurrent dreams about people waking me up and telling me it is time to go to the hospital to have the transplant add to my anxiety. How am I going to live on the edge like this for another six weeks?

Then the beeper goes off again. "Holy Shit!" I scream aloud. The transplant staff told me they would beep me twice. This can't be real. My name was placed on the UNOS list on Thursday, and it is Sunday night. It's only been three days! It isn't my time. I'm not ready. I need two more weeks. Okay, one more week. There is so much still left to do. I start shaking like a leaf.

LERITA: Harvey, oh Heavy? Are they calling us?
HH: 'Fraid so, Lerita. This is it.

LERITA: (Screaming) NO, NO, I'M NOT READY! YOU CAN'T LEAVE ME YET! THEY SAID FOUR TO SIX WEEKS!

HH: Lerita, please calm down and quit screaming. There is no one here but us. I can hear you.

LERITA: No, No. I'm not ready.

HH: But you have to be, Lerita. They have a heart for you.

LERITA: What about next month? They said four to six weeks!

HH: Lerita, events like this do not follow the laws of time. They follow the laws of God.

LERITA: God? What does God have to do with this? I mean, why is God letting this happen?

HH: You are losing it, and this is really not the time. There are many things that you don't understand. However, if you insist on a lecture, there are all kinds of laws that we've created in the world to make sense of everything. There are laws of time, of economics, of medicine. Things like transplants, people having accidents and families donating their organs don't follow rational laws. I'm afraid this one is not your call; it's out of your control. It's the beginning of the road of trust we talked about. It is the road you are going to have to journey on from this point. Now if you would just...

LERITA: I don't want you to go. You can't go yet. We haven't finished talking and sharing and, ...

HH: I'm so sorry, Lerita, I really love you, and that is why I must leave now. To be quite honest, I don't have much more time.

LERITA: WHAT?

HH: I know the doctors said we might have 18 months together but that was their diagnosis based on your previous echocardiograms. As you will learn, physicians aren't always accurate in their prognostications. I started slowing down about three years ago, and I just keep getting *slower* and *slower*. I have shifts too, and in a couple of weeks, there will be a big one—more like a tidal wave. It's coming, and I'll be barely pumping. They would have to rush you to the hospital, and you would be on a pump until a heart became available and I might not be able to hold out. I don't think you want that, so I suggest you get on the phone to Margaret and tell her you are coming in for that new heart.

LERITA: Harvey no! I won't do it!

HH: Oh yes you will. There are too many people counting on you, Lerita, for you to do something so foolish as to pass up a new heart to keep an old one that is failing.

LERITA: But what will you do?

HH: I'll teach many young doctors and scientists a great deal about heart disease. I'll be able to help thousands of patients who have heart problems similar to yours. How do you think they know so much about your IHSS? A lot of new information comes from examining worn-out hearts like me. Right now, though, I want you to pick up that phone and call Margaret.

LERITA: No, no. I'm not going to let them take you. We can die together.

HH: And what purpose would that serve? Can't you see how much good you can do by staying alive? Do you realize how many people have benefited from your presence on earth? We could start with the students you've taught over the past 15 years. We don't have time to discuss the friends and family who look to you for spiritual insight. Lerita, you still have a lot of work to do. There is a purpose for your life and you must remain alive. You must have this transplant so that others will be strengthened by your courage and resolve to live life and live it to the fullest. You've got to share the knowledge you've gained in these conversations by writing about them. You will provide inspiration for others. Trust me. I know, and I speak for the Wisdom of the Ages. It's not your time. You must remain ALIVE.

LERITA: I don't want to live.

HH: Lerita, this is not the time for your melodrama. You're squandering precious time that we could be using to say good-bye.

LERITA: (Sobbing) Oh no.

HH: LERITA, GET A GRIP. I KNOW YOU CAN BE CALM. THIS IS NO TIME TO BE FALLING APART. YOU ARE GOING TO NEED STRENGTH TO GET THROUGH THE SURGERY. You are not in charge of this part. You are going to have a heart transplant within the next 12-18 hours. It's reality time. Let's go. Take three deep breaths and dial that phone.

LERITA: (Breathing deeply) That does feel better. Oh Heavy, I don't think I can do this.

HH: Can do! Will do! Do you think I've been wasting my limited energy these past few months for nothing?

LERITA: We have talked a great deal, and I know you better. How can you leave?

HH: I've been trying to prepare for this moment, Lerita. I'm sure our conversations helped both of us to get ready. Now it's time to get the show on the road. We are having a transplant if I have to drag you to the hospital myself.

LERITA: How do you plan to do that?

HH: I have my ways.

LERITA: Like what? Ah ...Oh, that's a pain in my chest. Oh. It hurts. Oh my God!

HH: You want more? I can make it worse.

LERITA: I cannot believe you're doing this. Oh, you're hurting me!

HH: I cannot believe I have to do this. My God, you are stubborn. Get to the phone. I promise, after you speak with everyone, we'll talk more. We'll have our last heart-to-heart talk.

LERITA: (Sobbing) I am going to miss you so much...

HH: Please don't get started again. You need to be composed on the phone.

LERITA: OK, OK. This isn't the final goodbye?

HH: We'll have time to talk while you're waiting on your ride. First things first.

I start searching for the list of numbers I had prepared. Somehow, though, I cannot seem to locate the number for the transplant coordinator, Margaret Waller, or the hospital. I end up scanning the yellow pages for University Hospital's number. Hands trembling, I dial the number and ask them to page the heart transplant coordinator. Margaret comes on the line. "Lerita, how are you?" *How am I? I am scared shitless.* I reply, "Uh, okay, I guess. Did you beep me?"

"As a matter of fact, I did. I think we have a heart for you," she says.

"This soon? I've only been on the list for 3 ½ days!" I say, expressing my utter disbelief.

"I know that. This is highly unusual, but it looks like a 90 percent go. Do you think you can get to the hospital in the next hour?"

Although I tell her I am on my way, I am still unprepared for a heart transplant and definitely not willing to let Heavy Harvey go yet.

LERITA: OK. That's done. I still don't believe this. We had all of these conversations so I would be prepared but I am not ready after all.

HH: Think about what you would have been like if we had not talked.

LERITA: What final things do you need to tell me?

HH: Not so fast. Where is that transplant telephone tree list you made up, "Ms. Always Organized?" You've got five other people to call, get your bag, and check the thermostat. You know you won't be home for a while.

LERITA: It wasn't supposed to happen like this. I don't have my e-mail list for Hank, and I don't know who is going to teach my classes. What about the license plates for the car, and...?

HH: Hold on. Aren't you forgetting about priorities here? If you don't have a ticking heart, none of this other stuff matters. You're a goner. Finis. Lerita, I don't want to get tough with you, especially now because I know you're terrified and we're parting, but you must make those phone calls. QUIT STALLING.

LERITA: Oh, all right. I guess I better start with my ride. I sure hate to wake up Mom and Dad in the middle of the night.

HH: They'll be OK. Let's go.

I call the five people at the top of my transplant contact list, and they all answer except for Gail. I tell them I have been beeped and it is time to head for the hospital. I notify Mom and Dad last.

LERITA: Mom and Dad are in shock.

HH: It's not surprising. You are too. Boy, I thought I was going to have to go into full cardiac arrest in order to get you to pick up the phone. Let's go through the checklist. You have your hospital bag, and I've got the stuff you want me to take. It took a moving van.

LERITA: Thanks a lot.

HH: Just a little heart humor. You need some right now. Have your journal?

LERITA: Oh yes. This experience is certainly worth some serious self-reflection and perhaps a story. I checked the thermostat, and the doors are locked. Why is this happening now?

HH: Because it is necessary.

LERITA: How profound.

HH: Getting sarcastic on me, huh? Been there. Heard that.

LERITA: You're mighty feisty in the early morning.

HH: You keep forgetting. I never sleep. I may slow down a bit, but sleep is not a part of my job description.

LERITA: Oh, what am I going to do with someone else's heart?

HH: You are going to do just fine, Lerita. How many times do I have to tell you that you'll have a new life? You'll be able to live in ways you have never lived before so don't waste it.

LERITA: Waste it? How could I waste it? Have I ever wasted my life?

HH: Need I mention the drinking during your freshman year in college as in "getting wasted?" Thank God you only smoked cigarettes for two weeks. Then there is food...

LERITA: I rarely eat junk food.

HH: That's only a recent improvement. Most important, be careful about who you open up your heart to.

LERITA: Open up my heart to? You mean as in romance?

HH: Yes. You tend to give your heart away too quickly and to every Tom, Dick and Harry who's single and looks like good husband material.

LERITA: I am not *that* bad.

HH: Lerita, how many times have you had your heart broken because you gave it to someone who either didn't want it or didn't know how to care for it?

LERITA: How am I supposed to know?

HH: Do I have to be specific?

LERITA: Yes.

HH: You must trust your heart only to a trustworthy person. Remember the key word here is TRUST-worthy, worthy of your trust. You can't know if someone is trustworthy unless you take time to get to know him.

LERITA: I must admit I am usually in a rush when I meet someone I like. It's harder now that I am over 40. Will I ever find Prince Charming or Mr. Right?

HH: Isn't that backwards? Didn't Prince Charming *find* Sleeping Beauty? You're a treasure. You should let him find you.

LERITA: I can't remember, and we may be mixing up Sleeping Beauty with Cinderella. In both cases, though, now that you mention it, the guys came looking for the women. I get lonely sometimes, and I miss having companionship.

HH: When did you lack friends?

LERITA: It's not the same as having someone special.

HH: Your social calendar is quite extensive. In fact, you could cut back a bit.

LERITA: That's true. Sometimes I'm not certain if I am coming or going.

HH: Recovering from a heart transplant will help you put the brakes on all those social activities.

LERITA: Really?

HH: You don't think you are going to get off the table and walk out of the hospital do you? It's going to be a long haul, Lerita. The rest of the body, especially the immune system, has got to adjust to having a new heart. It won't be easy.

LERITA: When will it all be over?

HH: It will be over when it's done.

LERITA: Thank you very much, Mr. Heavy Harvey.

HH: I don't think this is the time for us to be getting testy with each other. There's not much time left, and I've got several things I want to share with you before I'm gone for good.

LERITA: I still cannot believe that this is our final conversation. Boy, that packing stuff was painful. I didn't know I had been carrying around such a load of ugly stuff. Is there anything else you need to tell me before you leave?

HH: Well your recovery will take longer than you think.

LERITA: They say I'll be back to work in about three to four months.

HH: Let me repeat myself. Your recovery will take longer than you think—than you want. You won't be happy about it, but in the long run, you'll understand why it took so long. Remember, patience is golden, "Miss Always Wannabe in Control."

LERITA: Man, thanks a lot.

HH: You're welcome. Really, Lerita, like I said before, it will be a lesson in balance. It is important to know when to surrender and when to take the bull by the horns. It's an ability few people develop, let alone master. It's tied to listening to the Voice.

LERITA: I got it.

HH: You *will* get it before it is all over.

LERITA: What kind of vote of confidence is that?

HH: (Hearing doorbell) It's your ride. Rose, Jean and Liz Beth are here to take you to the hospital.

LERITA: OK. Let's see, where is my bag? Do you have all the things that you're taking? Oh, I don't think I am ready for this.

HH: Sounds like you are stalling again.

LERITA: I thought we would have more time.

HH: I answered all of your questions, didn't I?

LERITA: Yes, I'd say you have given me more than enough guidance.

HH: Lerita, I do have a final bit of advice.

LERITA: What is that?

HH: Remember these four words: LISTEN, TRUST, PATIENCE, and SURRENDER.

LERITA: LISTEN, TRUST, PATIENCE and SURRENDER. I think I can remember that.

HH: In order to maneuver through this transplant and the rest of your life with a joyful heart, you are going to have to LISTEN to the quiet urgings of your spirit that lies deep within your heart. You are going to have to TRUST what it tells you. You're going to need plenty of PATIENCE. And you are going to have to relinquish some of that control you love so much; that's where the SURRENDER comes in. You are not directing this transplant. That is why you are being called only four days after being placed on the list! It is an omen—a big signal to you that YOU ARE NOT IN CHARGE OF THIS. Please try to go with the flow. I know it will be difficult for you since we know how much you like to run things.

LERITA: I don't try to run everything.

HH: Weren't you planning to teach the first three weeks of the semester and have the transplant sometime in early February?

LERITA: Yes, I thought that was how it would turn out.

HH: And you don't want to be in control? Anyway, as I was saying, it is important for you to *listen* but we've talked about that already.

LERITA: Is something bad going to happen?

HH: No. I don't want to frighten you. There are lots of messages that need to be passed through you and they won't get out there unless you learn to listen better. Then you've got to *act*—to trust what you hear. The messages won't always come in words—they'll be more like gentle urges. Notice that most successful people know how to use their spiritual resources. They know how to listen to an inner guide that leads them through the maze of life. You've done fairly well so far. We both know that by being *still* and listening to the little Voice, you've been guided through college, graduate school, open-heart surgery, three academic positions, and buying two houses. You understand that. But you still possess this need to control and do it *your* way. If you want your recovery to go smoothly, you must *listen* and *trust*. You'll be able to hear better now because your heart space is clear for your new heart.

LERITA: Is there anything else?

HH: I cannot overemphasize it. Doctors make mistakes. They are human and not every*body* follows the formulas in their medical books. There will be some "oops-ing" and it is very important for you to pay attention to your inner guidance. You're also going to be a little more terrified than usual because you'll be navigating new territory. You've never had a transplant before, and with all of the medications and side effects, it will be like moving to a new country.

LERITA: I don't think I like the way this sounds. Am I going to die?

HH: Trust me. This is not your time. Just be sure to listen.

LERITA: I can hear the Voice, but following it all of the time is challenging.

HH: Remember that Spirit is always conveying messages. Do the best you can; quieting the inside chatter and the external noise will help tremendously. It is okay to be reclusive while you are recovering. You don't have to socialize. In fact, isolation is important. Be selective about the company you keep, if you keep any company at all, because people will drain you of the energy you need to heal. And, if your gut tells you to do something like "call the doctor," don't second-guess it. Just do it.

LERITA: What's going to happen now?

HH: You need to answer the door, gather your things, and report to University Hospital. There they will prep you for the surgery, knock you out, take me out and put your new heart in.

LERITA: You make it sound so matter of fact. Aren't you going to miss me?

HH: Yes, Lerita I am. I am going to miss you terribly. I love you. I've always loved you and I cannot think of a better way of showing you than this. I've tried to keep beating as long as I can. Remember, I have only about two weeks left.

LERITA: You mean if this heart hadn't arrived in time you would have stopped on me and I would have died?

HH: Lerita, you've got to remain calm. If you don't, I'll have to beat harder and I could stop all of a sudden.

LERITA: Oh, I'm sorry. I didn't mean to get upset.

HH: I want to emphasize three things. First, God cares for you, Lerita. Don't forget that spiritual, "His Eye is On the Sparrow." Will you promise me that you'll remember that?

LERITA: Yes, I promise, Heavy.

HH: Second, the heart is connected to your Spirit and your heart's desires are *influenced* by what is in your heart. Things like emotional pain, anger, jealousy and disappointment affect what you think you want and what you believe your heart is telling you.

LERITA: How am I supposed to tell the difference?

HH: By the amount of inner peace and joy you feel. There is a qualitatively different feeling about inner joy and euphoria. Driving a new car, being infatuated or winning an award can all bring about a euphoric feeling, but it's temporary. Inner joy only seems temporary but that's because negative feelings like anger and disappointment subdue it...

LERITA: Jealousy, envy, shame, anger, disappointment... I got it.

HH: Third, the universe operates under different laws than the ones you've learned. That's why you were directed to go on the list right after the holidays. That is why the Voice told you that waiting to have a transplant until the end of the academic year in May was insane. There are no accidents, Lerita. All of this is supposed to happen but, as you can see, it is not following what you thought was the normal course of things. I've known for some time that you would be called tonight. But I didn't have the heart to tell you.

LERITA: This is no time for a heart pun!

HH: Sorry. Besides, I wasn't intending that one. I knew that you were not ready to hear about it when I got the message.

LERITA: I understand.

HH: OK, I believe you're ready.

LERITA: I guess this is it, huh?

HH: Yes, Lerita.

LERITA: I don't want to say goodbye. I need more time to say all of the things I should have said 10, 20 years ago, like thank you for keeping me alive, or, remember the time when we were in London and we had an arrhythmia attack after I drank too much tea, but you saw me through—all of those things. Time has run out. Soon you'll be gone forever.

HH: At least we have this time together, Lerita. Some people don't get an opportunity to say goodbye to someone they love. They don't have a chance to tell them anything. Think about all of the accidents and sudden deaths. As the phrase goes, "Tomorrow is not promised." I hope you will remember this lesson.

LERITA: Lesson?

HH: Yes, tell the people you love that you love them *now*. Let them know how much you appreciate them *now*. Forgive whomever you need to forgive *now*. If you have hate in your heart for someone, work on it *now*. Try to clear the air. It's so much more difficult to deal with these affairs of the heart after someone dies or is no longer available to receive and respond to your words. Don't wait to talk with Mom and Dad or your sister or brothers or your friends or colleagues. Everything and everyone is on loan. Nothing in this world will last and that is especially true of relationships. When you die, you can't take anyone with you.

LERITA: Heavy, you have taught me so much. I didn't realize that hearts carry such wisdom in addition to all of the emotional material. I wish I had talked with you earlier so I could avoid this, this loss.

HH: People rarely consult their hearts even when there is a major crisis. Instead, they check their astrological charts, stock reports, and previous studies. Who stops to listen from within or attempts to talk to their hearts about what to say, where to go, or what to do? You are way ahead of the curve in this domain, Lerita.

LERITA: Okay, Heavy. I know you think *I* am ready and possibly I am ready but I have a few things I need to say.

HH: Oh really?

LERITA: It's always been hard for me to say this—by the way, why is it so much harder to say, "I love you" than "I hate you?"

HH: It has to do with maintaining autonomy and separation. Hating someone allows you to disconnect, but when you say you love someone, it automatically pulls you closer. Most human beings actually fear *real* love; they fear the deep connection that comes with true intimacy. To be and feel connected is a natural state for spirits, but not for bodies. That's why most relationships are colored by ambivalence.

LERITA: You could have been a psycho-theological professor with an explanation like that. So I'm a spirit?

HH: You'll internalize that lesson on the next phase of this journey. Yes, Lerita, as I've mentioned before, you are a spirit, not a body. But you were about to say?

LERITA: (Sobbing) I'm going to miss you so much. I can't imagine how I am going to live without you and especially with a strange, or should I say different, heart. You've assured me that I will be OK. I'm not sure I believe it. I am so sorry you're leaving and I won't be able to talk to you anymore.

HH: Here, let me give you a hug.

LERITA: There's that warm and fuzzy heart-warming feeling again. It feels so good.

HH: Well it's straight from the heart.

LERITA: I can't believe it. Heart puns til the end.

HH: You're smiling. It's time to get going, Lerita. One more hug together.

LERITA: (Sobbing again) Oh, Heavy...

HH: Keep playing that first song on the Whitney Houston *Bodyguard* soundtrack, OK?

LERITA: What song is that?

HH: Don't worry about it now. Listen to it as often as you can. Good-bye, Lerita.

LERITA: Good-bye, Heavy. I'll see you in heaven.

HH: Yes, we'll be together again someday. Be sweet.

LERITA: Heavy, Heavy...

HH: (no answer)

LERITA: Heavy, I want to tell you one more thing.

HH: (no answer)

LERITA: Heavy? Wait. Come back. I want to tell you one more thing!

HH: (no answer)

LERITA: Heavy? Please answer. Heavy, are you there? I want to tell you that I love you!!

HH: (no answer)

LERITA: (Sobbing heavily) Oh my God. He's gone. He's really gone.

I answered the door, and there stood Rose, Liz Beth and Jean shivering in the frosty January air. We gathered up my things, and on Monday morning, January 9, 1995, at University Hospital in Denver, Colorado, they cut Heavy Harvey out and replaced him with a new heart. Immediately, Heavy was sent to the pathology lab where samples and slides were made. Due to his enormous size (it was described as one of the largest hearts ever seen at University Hospital), he began teaching the medical profession and the science community alike about cardiomyopathy. His pictures and echocardiograms became a major teaching tool for medical students, residents, and geneticists, even contributing to the genome project. His greater gift, his wisdom, will remain with me forever.

Reflections

Is there anything preventing you from hearing the wisdom of your heart?

Is there anyone that you need to say "I love you" to right now?

If you have ever had an injury, illness or disease, what do you think the illness was trying to teach you (e.g., are heart problems teaching you about being more loving; kidney issues speaking to you about eliminating toxins from your life; or neurological issues urging you to change the way you think about things)?

PART 2
Hope for a New Day
Day of the Transplant...

This message appeared in emails to the Department of Psychology faculty and staff and 125 people on "Lerita-list" on January 9, 1995.

> To: lerita-list@psych.col.edu, faculty@psych.col.edu, staff@psych.col.edu,
> From: Hank Richardson <Hank.Richardson@Col.EDU>
> Date: Monday, 09 Jan 1995 22:34:32 -0700 (MST)
> Subject: Lerita (recovery room update)

Lerita is just starting to wake up, but a few friends were allowed in to see her. They had been warned in the transplant handbook that it was not unusual for patients to accumulate as much as 10 pounds of liquids during surgery and that this sometimes makes patients almost unrecognizable to their friends and family. Those who saw Lerita report the opposite. She looks better than before surgery. And most importantly, with all the monitors, it is easy to see the strong, regular heartbeat. The surgeon said not a single thing went wrong during the surgery, which is most unusual in something this complicated. Questions you've asked:

The donor? We know nothing specific about the donor except that he/she donated a heart to Lerita, a liver to someone else, and a kidney to each of two people. A nurse involved in the "harvesting" reported that Lerita got an excellent, strong heart. She may be supercharged. This may be a good time for all of us who are grateful for Lerita's new heart to make sure that our own donor cards are up-to-date. Writing to Lerita? She hasn't landed anywhere semi-permanent yet, so cards and letters would likely get lost in the maze of University Hospital. I'll have more info on this tomorrow. I can easily print out your email messages and have them taken to the hospital if you wish. The summary from everyone at the hospital is that it could not possibly have gone any better.

Hank

Awake again, fuzzy arrays of recognizable people appear by my bedside from time-to-time. I think I see Martha, Liz Beth, Jean, and my parents. That one looks like Martha's friend, Brenda, from book club. How did she get in here? Maybe they thought she was my sister. My brother Kenneth is here? Ooh, I hope I didn't die. I didn't expect him to show up! I've never seen him leave work for anything, and given the contentious nature of our relationship... Can that really be him?

Although I've awakened from open-heart surgery in an ICU before, this time it is different. My first clear thoughts are, "Wow, I survived a heart transplant! I can't believe it!" As is typically the case, there are wires and tubes everywhere. Machines beep, monitors light up the otherwise cavernous scene of an ICU cubbyhole. Catheters and IV's tag my body like a dartboard. Then there is the dreaded intubation tube that I hate more than anything. I try to sleep through the constant gag reflex, sore throat, and difficulty swallowing. I look over at the nurse nearby who continues to write numbers from the various blinking monitors on a chart. I want to communicate the question, "How long do I have to deal with this tube?" when I feel my body start to move uncontrollably. *Are we having an earthquake?* My eyes must express the terror when the nurse serenely says, "Ms. Coleman, you are having a seizure. Try to remain calm." Other nurses and doctors rush into the room as my body flops on the bed like a beached whale. Panic thoughts prevail. *I've had this heart for less than 24 hours, and I am having a seizure! Is this what my life is going to be like now? How is this going to affect my brain, my cognitive abilities? I'm a professor; I have to be able to think!*

Rigid yet unable to move, I feel my body settle down on the bed sheets. "Ms. Coleman, you just had a seizure, but you are going to be okay. This is not an uncommon reaction to the strong anti-rejection drugs you were given for the transplant. Try to relax," she says again. *Thank God for nurses.*

I need Heavy. He can explain to me what to do now. Then it dawns on me. Heavy is gone. He's not here to offer any guidance. I could talk to this new heart, but I don't think I am up to talking after that emotionally gut-wrenching goodbye with Heavy. How do I approach a conversation with a heart that has been in my body for less than 24 hours? It feels like walking up to a stranger on the street and asking if they would like to get some coffee?" Awkward cannot begin to describe the circumstances. Yet I am desperate because who knows what will happen next in the ICU. I muddle through my first attempt to contact my new heart.

LERITA: (Gently) Hello?

(No answer)

LERITA: Hel-lo.

(No answer)

LERITA: Hel-lo. I know you're there. I feel a heartbeat.

(No answer)

LERITA: *Please* answer.

(No answer)

LERITA: How about a quiet "Hi" or respond in any way that you can?

HEART: Hi? (Softly)

LERITA: Oh. You *are* there.

HEART: (Silence)

LERITA: I only want to say hello and welcome.

HEART: (Whispering) Welcome?

LERITA: I know this may seem weird to you but….

HEART: (Whispering) Who are you and why are you trying to talk to me?

LERITA: (Laughing) I'm sorry. I didn't mean to frighten you. How about if I tell you some of my story, and when we talk again you can tell me about your life before, we uh, met.

HEART: (Still whispering) Whaat?

LERITA: Yes, it is such an incredible tale. I'm not sure where to start. I'd better start with where I left off.

HEART: Where you left off?

LERITA: I'm sorry. I know it's confusing. I had this sick heart named Heavy Harvey.

HEART: Heavy?

LERITA: Yes, Heavy Harvey. Yes, well, I didn't know his name was Heavy at first, but we got to talking...

HEART: You actually *talked* to your heart like *this*?

LERITA: Didn't you talk to the last person you were with?

HEART: Talk with? No. We communicated sometimes.

LERITA: You never conversed?

HEART: Not like this.

LERITA: What do you mean not like this?

HEART: We did not speak in words—feelings and thoughts sometimes, but no talking.

LERITA: I see. We, that's Heavy Harvey and I, didn't talk until near the end, during the final weeks before he left.

HEART: He? Your heart had a gender, and he left?

LERITA: Yes, kind of, well, Heavy had a masculine tone. Anyway, we talked over the course of several weeks before he left, uh, before they removed him from my body.

HEART: I'm sorry.

LERITA: Thanks. When the beeper went off the final night, I didn't know it was going to be the final conversation.

HEART: You had more than one of these talks?

LERITA: (Sobbing) It was such an experience. I can hardly find the words to describe what I learned from my precious heart.

HEART: It sounds like you're very sad.

LERITA: (Still sobbing) Yes. I miss Heavy a lot. He had incredible wisdom.

HEART: Why did he leave or why did they take him from you?

LERITA: A terrible disease called IHSS killed him. The disease resulted from a genetic disorder.

HEART: Oh.

LERITA: He began to slow down, and would have eventually stopped. We both would have died if they had not performed a heart transplant and found you to take his place.

HEART: Oh my.

LERITA: So thank you.

HEART: I'm not sure how I was chosen for you, but I don't mind helping out. Alright, nice meeting you, uh…?

LERITA: Lerita. My name is Lerita.

HEART: Nice talking to you, Lerita.

LERITA: Same here. Can we talk again soon?

HEART: Okay maybe.

Reflections

Do you embrace change? When major changes happen in your life, how do you usually respond?

Do you think your heart is open enough to have a conversation? Why or why not?

Could a traumatic event like a life-threatening illness, loss of a loved one, or of a job trigger a conversation with your heart?

Getting Acquainted
About two weeks after the transplant...

Released from the hospital just 12 days following the heart transplant, I feel a surreal sense of accomplishment and devastation simultaneously. I survived a heart transplant and, in record time, I am back in my lovely townhome gazing at Boulder's picturesque Flatirons Mountain perched right outside my window. Unfortunately, as I settle into the comfort and familiarity of my own bed with my favorite comforter, two pillows and Laura Ashley floral sheets, I experience recurrent bouts of tachycardia, a major sign of heart transplant rejection. I try to ignore these sudden, racing heartbeats, but the episodes increase in frequency and length. They steal my breath, cause extreme dizziness and elicit a core body panic. My thoughts race: "What is happening? Am I going to be able to keep this heart? Is this what my new life is going to be like?" I procrastinate as long as I can. Fearing that I will lose consciousness during a tachycardia episode, I reluctantly call the transplant coordinator, who advises me to report to the hospital immediately. Once admitted and stabilized, I decide to send an email to all of my friends, family and colleagues. I hope writing will distract me from the terror and malaise setting in.

To: lerita-list@psych.col.edu, faculty@psych.col.edu, staff@psych.col.edu
From: LERITA@clipr.col.edu
Date: Fri, 27 January 1995 18:29:32 -0700 (MST)
Subject: Update on Lerita from Lerita
Hello Everyone,

First, I want to thank all of you for the prayers, positive thoughts, good vibes, and especially for the contributions to my medication fund. Gail told me that it is nearly $2,000 and I was so overjoyed that I cried. It's becoming increasingly clear that I will need all of the help I can get with these very expensive transplant medications.

Yes, I am back in University Hospital, and I hear that some of you are worried. Please don't be. I was readmitted for a rejection episode, which is very common during the first three months. In fact, not to have rejection is atypical.

Women are more likely to experience rejection with organs (at least with hearts) than men. They believe it is because women bear children and their immune systems may be structured or operate differently than men. One reason I was on the list for only four days is because of my petite body size, A+ blood type and living in this region of the country with a high donor rate and distance from other transplant centers. Next, doctors match donor and recipients on HLA/DNA tissue type (antigens). The matching on tissue type involves a set of six antigens. If you match on all of them, you would have no rejection, but it is likely they gave you your old organ back. (You should laugh here.) Or, if they match four or five antigens, it probably means that the donor is more related to you than you thought. Recently a man in Michigan received his daughter's heart and, although he suffered serious emotional anguish, he did not experience any rejection. Sometimes more rejection occurs when the match is cross-gender rather than same-gender. I now know that my donor was a 40-year-old white female. Yes, I know, and I did ask why I didn't receive the heart of a 19-year-old! My doctor said a good heart is a good heart and sometimes they transplant hearts of older people into other older people.

The current course of anti-rejection treatment lasts about 10 days, so I will be in the hospital for at least that amount of time. After the first few treatments, the echocardiograms of my heart showed signs that my heart is pumping better. Another biopsy early next week will confirm my progress. Note that this may not be my last visit to the hospital, although things should smooth out as time passes. Hopefully, my next report will be from home. I look forward to limited visits soon.

Lerita

The note sounds far more upbeat than I feel. Today, as I recline in my hospital bed, I sense that it is time for another talk with my new heart. *My heart?* I don't think I can claim this heart of two weeks as mine. Yet I know that my body, especially this heart, is struggling. I will be in the hospital for weeks, reeking with steroids and God knows what else unless I establish some rapport.

LERITA: Hello again.

HEART: (Silence)

LERITA: Hi there. Hello, new heart.

HEART: (Softly) Good morning? I'm not sure how this talking business works.

LERITA: It is like a friendly conversation.

HEART: Yes, but we are not friends. I don't know you.

LERITA: I know. The getting-acquainted process is a little awkward. We could start by having you talk about the person you were with before. You must miss, uh....

HEART: Jody Goetz.

LERITA: Jody. Yes, I heard that my organ donor was a woman. So you lived in a woman's body?

HEART: Yes. She was wonderful. It is very strange to be with, or should I say beating, inside of another person. (Sighing) I guess we're here together now.

LERITA: I have so much to be thankful for. I waited only four days!

HEART: That is a miracle.

LERITA: What else can you tell me about Jody?

HEART: (Slowly and sadly) Jody, oh she was so sweet and loving. She had a lot of gusto and she would try anything once. She was a big football fan; Green Bay Packers and LA Raiders were her favorite teams. She loved her cats dearly.

LERITA: Jody and I have some things in common. I am a big football fan too, although I like watching college more than pro. I don't have any pets. Well, I had a dog, Dizzy, but I didn't have the energy to keep up with him once I started moving in and out of heart failure.

HEART: I am so upset that Jody was struck down in the prime of her life.

LERITA: It sounds very tragic.

HEART: Yes, it is a very tragic story. She had a brain aneurysm.

LERITA: A brain aneurysm? She wasn't very old, was she?

HEART: She just turned 40. Jody hung out with her best friend, Cathy, for New Year's Eve. Cathy fixed a great meal of ribeye steak and crab legs. They watched some stupid movie, laughed and went to bed. Jody got this horrendous headache, and on New Year's morning, she went home and got in bed. Sometime during the day, the pounding and pain got worse, and Jody knew something was terribly wrong. She tried to get up and reach for the phone, but she was too weak. Partially paralyzed, Jody fell out of the bed and landed underneath the ironing board, knocking the phone off the hook. She blacked out. I overheard the rest of the story in the ICU after Jody regained consciousness.

Cathy and Lillian, who was like a surrogate Mom for Jody, had planned a big surprise party to celebrate her 40th birthday on January 2nd. Cathy tried to call her several times and then came to the apartment with her spare key. When she arrived, Jody was on the floor having a seizure. Cathy called 911, and the paramedics took her and she ended up in the hospital's ICU.

LERITA: Oh no!

HEART: Jody worried incessantly as her birthday approached. She hoped she wouldn't have health problems in her 40's like her mom, who died from a brain tumor at 43 when Jody was only 12 years old.

LERITA: I am so sorry.

HEART: Thanks. She was in and out of consciousness for a couple of days, but Jody saw her Dad and two brothers, Cameron and Chris, before she suffered a massive stroke.

LERITA: Oh how sad.

HEART: Yes, with the drugs, the brain hemorrhaging, the shunt in the brain, I wasn't certain what was going on, but I knew it wasn't good. After the stroke, doctors informed Jody's family that she wasn't going to survive, so they agreed to donate her heart, two kidneys, her liver, some cornea and skin. Her dad was an optometrist, so he was happy that her eyes would help someone to see.

LERITA: I don't understand things like childhood cancer, sudden onset of a brain tumor in young adults, or my needing a heart transplant at age 41. It's such a mystery why there is so much physical suffering in the world. Yet look at the gift of life Jody gave to so many people, including me.

HEART: Yes, I'm not sure why Jody had to die. She was so full of life. It is wonderful that she could create new life for others.

Jody loved the outdoors and hoped to find a nice guy who liked to hike. She and Cathy were "single and hoping" as they described it. Even though they were unmarried women nearing their 40's, they still believed a happy marriage was coming. It's such a shame.

LERITA: I feel badly for her family. This transplant is so bittersweet. My family is rejoicing, and her family is in grief. I feel so conflicted.

HEART: You're right. It is very bittersweet.

LERITA: Now that you're here, I'm hoping to hike and ski. I could never do any of that—outdoor recreation—with my old heart. We were always sick.

HEART: Really? You mean you've never hiked in the majestic Rocky Mountains?

LERITA: No, I've always been a spectator from the car. I didn't have the stamina. My heart was too ill, and the higher altitude left me short of breath.

HEART: I'm starting to feel happy for you. There's so much you haven't seen, so much you've missed.

LERITA: I am certain there is. By the way, do you have a name?

HEART: It's Grace.

LERITA: Grace. That's a rather odd name for a heart, although I must admit until I met Heavy Harvey, I didn't realize hearts, or any organs for that matter, had names. Since you're Grace and Jody's last name was Goetz, I guess that would make you Grace Goetz. May I call you GG for short?

HEART: Yes, it's ok. As long as you remember that I'm Grace. It is quite an appropriate name in this situation, don't you think? Isn't this extension of your life an act of grace?

LERITA: Yes, it sure is.

GG: All right. What was your experience like on the day of the transplant?

LERITA: Actually, I was called about you in the middle of the night. My Boulder mothers—they're my "play mothers"—picked me up and drove me to the hospital. That's where the medical staff prepped me for surgery and rolled me into the OR.

GG: Were you afraid?

LERITA: I experienced more than a few moments of sheer terror, but thank God, Heavy Harvey prepared me. I'm not certain if I would have been ready without my conversations with him.

GG: Like I said before, this talking business is a little strange. I didn't have any conversations with Jody.

LERITA: I didn't talk to Heavy until I learned that I needed a new heart. I often wonder if I could have avoided the heart transplant if I had conversed with him sooner.

GG: Didn't he try to communicate with you before the end?

LERITA: He did say something about conveying certain feelings and sending red flags.

GG: Hmm. Did you pay attention?

LERITA: Did I pay attention to Heavy Harvey?

GG: Yes, did you listen to your heart before you two got sick?

LERITA: Sometimes. Now I realize that I was so busy with my life I rarely stopped to listen to my heart.

GG: That's too bad. I'm sure your heart was trying to guide you.

LERITA: Really?

GG: That's what hearts do besides other basic tasks like pumping and storing feelings.

LERITA: After my conversations with Heavy and losing him, I am definitely listening now.

GG: Is there anything else? Have we talked enough or are these conversations supposed to last longer?

LERITA: No. There's no set amount of time. But I have a serious problem I need to discuss.

GG: What's that?

LERITA: I'm in rejection.

GG: In rejection? What does that mean?

LERITA: My immune system does not recognize you as my heart, so it's on the attack. One of the symptoms is tachycardia which I felt a few days ago.

GG: Oh that. I was so frightened. I felt something attacking me. I started pumping harder hoping it might stop. Then I got a little drowsy. When I came to, everything seemed fine.

LERITA: Yes, the doctors gave me some medicine that would stop you from racing.

GG: Gee thanks.

LERITA: After they quieted you down, they started working on my immune system again. It is pretty unmanageable, and the doctors must use some very strong drugs to get it to retreat.

GG: Is that why it is so quiet?

LERITA: Basically. They're trying to calm it down permanently. It's not easy. You see I was very healthy when they sewed you in. Everything but my heart was in tip-top shape, including a very active immune system. It is the system that attacked you.

GG: What a word, "rejection."

LERITA: My friend Gail thinks "border disputes" is a better description.

GG: "Border disputes." That's cute.

LERITA: Sounds like human neighborhoods, huh?

GG: I suppose. Do I need to worry?

LERITA: I think the doctors are taking care of the problem with medications. I thought a heart talk might help.

GG: I see.

LERITA: You seem like a nice heart. You're very different from Heavy. I guess not all hearts are alike.

GG: Anatomically we look the same unless there is some abnormality. Since we live in such unique bodies, we do express ourselves differently.

115

LERITA: I could tell right away that you were quieter, a bit more reserved, than Heavy.

GG: Thank you. I hope that's a compliment.

LERITA: Yes, and an observation. Thanks for sharing some information about Jody. I didn't know what happened. I'll be seeing, I guess I should say, talking with you.

GG: That sounds fine. Am I supposed to say goodbye?

LERITA: No. How about, see you later?

GG: OK. Talk with you later.

Reflections

How do you become acquainted with new people?

What questions might you ask to become better acquainted with your heart?

How have you handled the loss of a loved one in your life? Did you find it difficult to accept it and move on?

Cultivating Patience
About three months after the transplant...

After a few weeks of mind-altering and physically draining medications in the hospital, I returned home feeling like an automobile on empty with absolutely no reserves. My home health care nurse reminds me that my recovery will take place one day at a time. But I want this daunting experience to be over NOW. I sit in my bed praying, "When will it be over?" and I hear Heavy Harvey's voice in my head, "It will be over when it's done." Oh, I miss my heart. But I keep praying. At least prayer is one thing that is familiar in this new transplant-recipient world.

Prayer is a funny thing. It has always been a part of my life. Prayer was an essential component of my life at St. Andrews Catholic School in Pasadena, California. We started the day with prayer. We ended the day with prayer. We prayed before and after recess. Prayer was required before and after lunch. And the prayers were repetitive. Same words. Same tone. "Bless me Father, for I have sinned...." "Hail Mary, full of grace..." It wasn't until I became an adult, until I started having needs that weren't reflected in these prayers that I learned how to pray with my heart. "Help me Lord. Please help me, Lord." "Please get me through these qualifying exams." "Can you help get this article published so I can get tenure?" "Is this the house for me, Lord?" "Will the finances work out?" "What are we going to do about this heart transplant, Lord? "Help me, Lord. Can you help me get through this ordeal?"

Despite my prayers, I am lost. I have no idea how to live this post-heart transplant life. It is such foreign territory. I feel like a woman running with the wolves, off in some South American jungle, following the Amazon wherever it might lead. I am not certain where I am going. I know I have a trusted and faithful Guide who keeps me out of serious danger and picks me up when I've grown too weary to keep moving. Sometimes I forget my Guide is there, though. It's odd. It is not as if it goes away. I merely forget.

I whine a lot about this adventure, and I wonder if having the transplant was the easiest or the hardest course? I sometimes question my faith. But I know I've got to have faith for life to be the daring adventure reflected in the

Helen Keller quote on the front of my journal: "Avoiding danger is no safer in the long run, than outright exposure. Life is either a daring adventure or nothing."

LERITA: Excuse me. Hello?

GG: (No answer)

LERITA: Grace?

GG: (No answer)

LERITA: Oh, Grace.

GG: Yes.

LERITA: Good. You answered. I need to talk with you.

GG: Really? I haven't heard from you in a while.

LERITA: I know. It's been rough. I thought I would be feeling a lot better by now. I haven't felt much like talking.

GG: I have this funny feeling that you are angry with me.

LERITA: Anger isn't what I'm feeling. I am upset, though, but it's not directed at you. Mostly I am tired of all of the side effects of the anti-rejection drugs. It didn't help that you had been exposed to the cytomegalovirus, and I hadn't. Despite all of the medications the doctors gave me to prevent it, I got it anyway. That meant more drugs.

GG: I'm very sorry about that.

LERITA: Sorry doesn't help much. I know it's not your fault.

GG: You're having a lot of trouble with this transplant aren't you?

LERITA: Yeah, I am.

GG: Do you regret your decision? Are you sorry that you decided to go through with it?

LERITA: If it had solely been my choice, or to put it another way, if I was writing my life's script, I don't think I would have included a heart transplant. I want to believe that some Higher Power, who knows better than I do, is in charge of this part.

GG: I am certain many people will be blessed by your journey.

LERITA: I hope something good comes out of this misery. I noticed that it was hard for me to contact you this morning.

GG: Really?

LERITA: It is uncomfortable to talk with someone I don't know very well. Now I know how you felt when I contacted you the first time. I was excited—happy to get through the surgery. I wanted to meet you and begin having a relationship. I didn't stop to think about how you might feel.

GG: I understand. Getting to know someone takes time.

LERITA: Yeah, we're actually in this for the long haul. It seems almost like a ...

GG: An arranged marriage?

LERITA: (Laughing) Of sorts. Yes. I didn't pick you and you didn't pick me but here we are together forever, I hope.

GG: You hope? Is there some doubt?

LERITA: I've heard about a few cases where people had so much rejection that they needed second and third hearts.

GG: Really? I cannot imagine going through all of this again.

LERITA: I don't want to think about it either. Let's switch topics. Uh, I had one item, but now possibly two I need help with.

GG: I'll try to do the best I can, but like I said before, I am still new to this chatting.

LERITA: I understand. You've been around for 40 years, though. I'm certain you are full of insights. Like you knew that I was having a hard time with the transplant recovery.

GG: Lerita, it is pretty clear you're having difficulty because you cry and whine about how bad it is to nearly anyone who will listen.

LERITA: I didn't think it would be so challenging.

GG: Why not? Didn't the nurses and other transplant recipients say it would be six months of hell?

LERITA: I heard that, but I guess I didn't believe them. Besides, I didn't know what they meant.

GG: It hasn't been so bad, has it?

LERITA: I guess it depends on your perspective. I have never felt so sick for such a long time. I am tired of stomach aches, headaches, ringing in my ears...

GG: Lerita. You don't have to go through the whole list, really you don't.

LERITA: Not very sympathetic, are you?

GG: I am not sure how I can help.

LERITA: It's OK. I had many conversations with Heavy Harvey about acting like a princess and being ungrateful.

GG: I don't think your struggle is about lacking gratitude. I understand how hard it must be for you to feel drugged, suffer through lots of side effects and not be able to keep up with your usual schedule. In some ways that may be good.

LERITA: Why is that?

GG: Did Heavy Harvey warn you about being too busy?

LERITA: We talked about how out-of-control my life was; how driven I was; and how having a transplant might help me feel the peace and joy I've sought for years.

GG: Could your illness be a blessing in disguise? It is allowing you time to change your life, similar to a grace period. Do you feel less driven since you had the transplant?

LERITA: Grace period? That's a good a pun, Grace. I don't know. I haven't made it out of the house yet. I am pretty much quarantined for about three months.

GG: Quarantined?

LERITA: Yes, I need to stay away from toddlers, crowds, airports, malls, and any place where there are lots of people, germs, or anything that could transmit a potential virus.

GG: I see.

LERITA: It's weird, though. I am allowed to go to the hospital for check-ups and biopsies—talk about a place full of germs! I am getting off track. I know I am living on borrowed time. I guess everyone is living on borrowed time, but to me, it seems more finite now. I figure if I have limited time, I don't want to spend it worrying. Now I need to have my best interests at heart. That's funny. Heavy Harvey always made heart puns, now I'm doing it.

GG: Lerita, there is something you need to know.

LERITA: What's that?

GG: I hate heart puns. All of them—what's in your heart, having your best interests at heart…

LERITA: I'm sorry. Why don't you like them?

GG: The heart is the most important organ that you have. I don't think anyone should make fun of it. It's your internal compass. It works with your spirit. It's both strong and delicate at the same time.

LERITA: What do you mean it's the most important organ?

GG: Lerita, you cannot live without it.

LERITA: I can't live without a liver or a brain either.

GG: That's true to an extent. You can have parts of your brain and liver missing and still live. There are some people with damaged hearts who manage to get around. But are there more people dying of liver and brain disease or heart problems?

LERITA: Touché. You got me with that one, Grace. You're quite a debater.

GG: Gee, thanks, but I wasn't trying to debate. I cannot overemphasize the importance of the heart. It is essential to everything that you experience.

LERITA: I guess I need to be more trusting with this heart transplant stuff?

GG: Yes, Lerita. Cultivating more trust would help us both at this point. Some patience would help too.

LERITA: Heavy Harvey named it as one of the big four.

GG: The big four?

LERITA: Yes, Heavy said there were four things that I need to master to get through the transplant, well, to get through the rest of my life too, "*Listen, trust, patience and surrender.*"

GG: It seems you've been doing fairly well with the first one, but the others are fairly problematic for you.

LERITA: I'm so tired of being a medical specimen. I must be the favorite case for medical rounds right now.

GG: All the more reason to be full of joy. Have you ever thought about all the people your case might help?

LERITA: Sort of, and I will probably be the subject of a few journal articles for some of those attending physicians.

GG: Isn't that great?

LERITA: What's so great about being the subject of medical research?

GG: Some doctor, some scientist, somewhere will be better equipped to treat the next generation of people with similar heart issues.

LERITA: Right.

GG: You are lighting the path for those who will follow.

LERITA: Yeah, right.

GG: Lerita, I may be a bit out of line here, but don't you think it is time to let go of some of your cynicism and pessimism?

LERITA: Do I sound cynical and pessimistic?

GG: Yes. Lerita, I don't know you very well, but your thoughts and actions speak for themselves. It's not that you portray yourself as a person with a high opinion of herself as a narcissistic person might, but not everything that happens in your life is about you. Sometimes you have to do things that you don't want to do because it's for the good of others, for a greater good. Are there people you admire, Lerita?

LERITA: You mean people that are alive?

GG: Yes, well, it doesn't matter if they are dead or alive.

LERITA: Let's see, there's Harriet Tubman, Mahatma Gandhi, Martin Luther King, Jr., Fannie Lou Hamer, Mother Theresa, Maya Angelou, August Wilson …

GG: Anybody living?

LERITA: My parents, Pope John Paul II, Oprah Winfrey and Colin Powell.

GG: Why do you admire them?

LERITA: They are talented. Their lives were or are devoted to doing something creative or constructive, like you said, for the greater good.

GG: Then I hope that you will think differently about all of the trials and tribulations that you're suffering through with the heart transplant. In every encounter you have, you can step beyond yourself; your life can touch someone else's.

LERITA: Heavy Harvey kept telling me the same thing. Is this some generic heart message?

GG: I don't think I would speak about it in that way. Love is the ultimate, the true emotion of the heart. It's being aware that your life and your experiences are much bigger than you. Love helps you understand that you are part of an interconnected web of relationships; it is designed to help you remember that everyone is connected. Love and connection are the universal message. Speaking of love, do you know how much you are loved, Lerita?

LERITA: I didn't give it much thought until I had the transplant

GG: Were you surprised?

LERITA: Yes, I was. It's not like people tell you every day that they love you, although maybe they should. It was more in how people acted toward me.

GG: How was that?

LERITA: For starters, when people heard I might need a transplant, some called to offer comfort and encouragement, others listened to me cry. I needed help getting through the shock of the diagnosis. My book club, Women of Words, gave me a beautiful painting of African-American women reading that I hung near my bedroom so I could be reminded of the better days ahead. Rebecca and Gail walked me through the transplant work-up. There were tons

123

of tests, and they turned them into humorous adventures. Martha held my hand as they wheeled me into surgery. Then there were the three Boulder "play" mothers—Rose, Liz Beth and Jean—who drove me to the hospital when I was beeped. They picked up Mom and Dad from the airport and stayed up for 24 hours until they knew that I survived the surgery.

Then Rebecca and Martha met me at the hospital in the middle of the night. They served as my advocates just in case I was unconscious and couldn't speak for myself. I got Rev. James, my associate pastor, out of bed at 3 a.m. to be with me in the surgery prep room. When I woke up from the surgery, I saw Kenneth, my brother, in ICU. I couldn't believe he would leave his job to come see me. Mom and Dad came to the hospital every single day, even during a Colorado freeze, and that was something considering that they are from California.

Gail set up a medication fund for me, and friends from around the country donated money. She wrote to them and asked them to write a check instead of sending flowers. That was phenomenal. It has made those trips to the pharmacy less stressful. I still don't understand why the drugs are so expensive and how pharmaceutical companies expect people to pay for them…

GG: I think you are getting sidetracked. You were speaking about the *love*.

LERITA: You're right. Mom was able to use that new family leave act and take off eight weeks from her job so she could take care of me. What a Godsend. My dear sweet friends from my old support group in Detroit—Harriet, Judy, June, Angela, Trudy, and Pam—each took a week off from work and used their vacation time to come and cook and care for me. My old college roommate, Peggy, flew in from South Carolina for another week. Friends at work, especially my assistant, Gloria, did all sorts of things; brought food and work to me at home, and drove me back and forth to the transplant clinic waiting through hours of tests and biopsies. Then there were the people who sent messages, movies, and books. I received over 175 cards, and each one felt like a spark of energy designed to keep me going when I had absolutely none. People everywhere are still praying for me, and my colleagues are teaching for me. Even Heathcliff picked me up and escorted me to an early morning transplant clinic visit. Heavy Harvey told me not to worry, but I never thought it would be so wonderful. I've been overwhelmed by the outpouring of love.

GG: That's what we are created to do, Lerita. That's why each person has a heart.

LERITA: To remind us to love?

GG: To move you, to urge you to love. To love is natural. It's the other stuff that gets in the way.

LERITA: Other stuff?

GG: Yes, things like anger, depression, anxiety and jealousy, things that keep you from thinking the loving thoughts and doing the loving things. We could spend the entire evening talking about love, but I think it may be time to end here.

LERITA: You're right, Grace. I think I'll go to bed so that we can get some rest. We will talk again later.

GG: Great.

Reflections

Who do you admire and why?

If you are ill or experiencing grief or trauma, how do you deal with the discomfort it causes?

Have you ever experienced grace in your life?

Do you know how much you are loved? How does this knowledge impact you?

The Stench
About five months after the transplant...

I truly want to live a normal life again. I took a sabbatical a couple of years ago, so this medical leave is truly unexpected. Each day I rise, and Mom or one of my dear girlfriends prepares breakfast. If I am not due for a clinic visit or blood work, I read and try not to worry about how much I am falling behind at work.

It seems strange to be on an extended leave without real plans. I cannot travel and daytime television filled primarily with soap operas and a few talk shows leaves me lacking. Occasionally, I catch The Oprah Winfrey or Sally Jesse Raphael shows. But many of the shows' storylines—molested children, boyfriends throwing lye on the faces of girlfriends, mothers stealing their daughter's boyfriends—are more than I can handle right now. I don't remember so much garbage on television in the past.

During my confinement, I spend a lot of time in the world of thought. I don't have the usual distractions of my routine tasks—grading papers, preparing lectures and manuscripts, and attending faculty and committee meetings. Now I am more aware of my obsessive thoughts about work. And without that distraction of work, I see the vapid wasteland of my life. I work, sleep, eat, watch television, go to church, and wish I were in a relationship. There must be more—there must be another way to be in the world.

I write in my journal that I want God, Jesus, the Holy Spirit, somebody to pull me out of the hell I've created in my mind and my heart. What drives me to be a workaholic, hold a Ph.D. from Harvard and still feel intellectually inadequate? Why am I angry with or possess great contempt for men? How can I have a lasting and loving relationship if I don't make a change in heart—an emotional transformation to go along with the physical one? Still, television dulls the pain and provides an escape from the existential crisis that my heart transplant presents. Lured into the fog of television watching, I fail to remember that I haven't talked to Grace in a while. I feel so ambivalent about contacting her. I want to talk to her about something other than how sick and miserable I feel. I don't want to appear ungrateful for my new life with my incessant complaints. I try to focus on love like she suggested.

I thought I learned all about hearts during my conversations with Heavy Harvey, but Grace is broadening my knowledge. As I begin my eighth week of procrastinating, I have a strange sensation that Grace is trying to contact me. That is almost too incredulous for me to fathom. But I realize she *is* calling me.

GG: Lerita.

LERITA: (no answer)

GG: Lerita.

LERITA: (no answer)

GG: Lerita!

LERITA: Grace, what is it? What's wrong?

GG: It stinks.

LERITA: What stinks?

GG: It stinks in here. The stench is horrible.

LERITA: Stench? Whatever are you talking about?

GG: The trash or garbage or whatever this stuff is that is piling up inside and all around me. It smells awful.

LERITA: Excuse me? What is it that smells? I know I've been watching some rubbish on television but does that seep into the heart space?

GG: Stuff like your anger and your disappointment does.

LERITA: You mean my emotions smell?

GG: Yes!

LERITA: What?! Heavy Harvey never mentioned that.

GG: Maybe he didn't have time. Perhaps it didn't matter to Mr. Harvey.

LERITA: Why?

GG: He was dying.

LERITA: That's heartless, Grace. What a terrible thing to say.

GG: Heart-less? Lerita, you know I don't like those heart puns.

LERITA: Sorry but it was the best description. Please don't talk like that about Heavy Harvey.

GG: Still a little attached to him?

LERITA: This is a side of you that I haven't seen. Are you jealous?

GG: Hardly. Why would I be jealous of Heavy Harvey?

LERITA: I don't know.

GG: I mean Heavy was so sick they had to get rid of him.

LERITA: So! Have you heard me say anything nasty about Jody?

GG: You couldn't say anything nasty. She was a wonderful person. Besides, I didn't say anything so awful about your old heart. And what I said was true.

LERITA: Where is all of this sarcasm coming from? Do you think Heavy put up with stinking emotions because he was dying? By the way, since when do emotions have aromas?

GG: I only get irritable when I am suffocating from the stench. This isn't just aroma, it's stench, like the smell of garbage. It's enough to make a heart want to stop beating. Resentment is the worst. It smells like garbage that has been sitting out in the hot sun for days.

LERITA: Really?

GG: Oh yes. That's because it keeps piling up. Would you like to talk about who or what you are resenting?

LERITA: It's some members of the transplant team. They get on my nerves.

GG: Why be resentful?

LERITA: It's a long story. It's one or two doctors, not all of them. They treat patients like objects, like a case number. Some think I should adore them because they are doctors. I can't stand it. I don't want to talk about it right now. Heavy mentioned that emotions can be noisy, but he said nothing about them smelling.

GG: Your ugly emotions can act as a blockage. Anger smells like burnt food— you know, how the house smells when you burn something.

LERITA: What about disappointment and depression?

GG: They stink too and are as bad as anger and resentment. Disappointment smells like the spray of skunk, though.

LERITA: Ugh.

GG: It's very bad in the beginning but typically dissolves over time.

LERITA: This is all so hard to believe.

GG: Believe it, ok? Depression is like disappointment, but basically, it smells like, well, uh...

LERITA: What, Grace? What does it smell like?

GG: Poop?

LERITA: You mean like feces?

GG: Yes. You know how intense that smell is, but it dissipates when it gets flushed.

LERITA: A little air freshener and a fan never hurt, either. What about a long-standing depression?

GG: I'm familiar with that. Jody was depressed sometimes. It smelled awful, worse than manure. I thought I might choke when she ignored it.

LERITA: What was the problem?

GG: She wasn't herself.

LERITA: What do you mean?

GG: Lerita, I know that you understand what I am talking about. Didn't I hear you say that you taught a course on the self-concept last semester? She developed a false self.

LERITA: Oh, yes. I know about them. I still struggle with mine. They are pretty common among certain types of depressives. The book *Drama of the Gifted Child* by Alice Miller helped me to understand myself. I felt like I wasn't good enough, so I unconsciously created a self that everyone would like. I became depressed because I was disconnected from who I truly am. Is that what happened to Jody?

GG: Somewhat, but Jody's circumstances were a bit different. She kind of shifted between depression and anxiety. I don't think Jody ever fully recovered from losing her mother at such a crucial time like adolescence. She was left as the only girl in a family of males who were preoccupied with men stuff. She tried to fit in, learned about how to be a cheese head—a big Green Bay Packers' fan—and all, but she really missed her mom. Having her best friend, Cathy, and her co-worker, Lillian, who was like a surrogate mother, helped Jody tremendously. Yet, Jody was pretty private and she didn't share everything with even her closest friends. She would occasionally talk with her brother, Cam, but she kept a lot inside. When the depression started, the smell was awful. I thought I might stop beating.

LERITA: Sounds unbearable.

GG: Yes, it can be. That's why it is so important to let stuff go regularly.

LERITA: Let what go?

GG: Whatever is bothering you. You know—the anger, resentment, depression, and disappointment.

LERITA: You make it sound so easy, Grace. It's not like holding some balloons in your hand and then deciding to let them go. It's hard to release some of those feelings, especially if I've had them for a long time.

GG: I know it's not simple, Lerita. But you need to know that it is impossible for me to sing and dance when the place smells like a dump. And when I sing...

LERITA: When you sing and dance, I feel joy.

GG: Yes, and I can continue to be Grace. Don't you think a sense of grace invokes deep joy? Besides, there are many ways of letting go of funky emotions, Lerita.

LERITA: That's true. Let's see I've prayed, used my journal, talked it out with friends like Jody did, joined a support group and got professional help. Some serious emotional problems require medication, though.

GG: I am glad you found some methods that helped.

LERITA: I remember in my 20s, I was so angry with my father that every time I spoke to him, my blood boiled.

GG: I told you anger smells like burnt food.

LERITA: Anger, boiling mad and burnt food. I never put them together.

GG: How did you let it go? Did you have close friends like Jody?

LERITA: Yes, but I didn't share a lot with my family and friends. I actually took the counseling route, and through that experience, I learned that I needed to forgive my dad.

GG: Hmm. Most people don't understand what that means.

LERITA: You're right, Grace. Dad didn't do anything malicious. He was emotionally unavailable, and as a child, I didn't have a name to describe the disconnection I felt. The frustration that emerged from my attempts to please him and from rarely receiving any affirmation led at first to anger and later to resentment. Then everything I perceived about him was filtered through the anger and resentment.

GG: So you let the resentment go?

LERITA: Definitely, although it took a good three years of asking Spirit to help me release it. I now know that beneath all of that anger was a lot of hurt.

GG: I bet you had been walking around with it for years.

LERITA: Yes, nearly 30 years.

GG: That's why it took so long, Lerita. When you hold on to resentment, it takes longer to release it from your heart.

LERITA: That makes sense. As a forgiveness practice, each time I felt the desire to lambaste Dad, I would say, "I forgive you, Dad" instead. I didn't think I would ever be able to think about him and feel neutral or positive, but one day I did. That's when I knew I was done; that I had actually forgiven him. Tell me, Grace, do positive feelings smell? How about joy, peace or compassion?

GG: Ah, now you are speaking of wonderful *aromas*, the smells that make me want to sing and dance. Joy is like a walk through a rose garden. The smell of beautiful roses is breathtaking don't you think? Even the leaves smell good.

LERITA: That's true. For me, the mere fact that a flower smells so aromatic is a miracle.

GG: Compassion smells like a freshly baked cake or bread, something made with lots of love. Peace is the evergreen pine of the forest. Have you ever walked in a forest? Those trees never lose their scent.

LERITA: I think I'm getting the picture. So, the negative emotions stink, and positive emotions smell like fragrances?

131

GG: Exactly. Think about it, Lerita. Have you heard of anyone trying to package the smell of garbage and sell it? Heard of a perfume called "Angry Heart" or "Maximum Depression?"

LERITA: (Laughing) Of course not.

GG: It's the wondrous times, the loving, joyful and peaceful times that fragrances are designed to remind us of.

LERITA: So you want me to get rid of the funky smells?

GG: Yes, please. The smell of roses, vibrant pines, and freshly baked cake or bread are so much better for you and me.

LERITA: I'll work on it, Grace. Like I said before, letting go of negative feelings is a process.

GG: I know you are quite capable, Lerita. If you would nip some of your funky attitudes in the bud before they bloom into...

LERITA: Sounds like a pun, Grace, nip-it-in-the bud, bloom?

GG: Some puns are ok. I don't like to joke about the heart. By the way, have you thought that there might be some relationship between your difficulties with organ rejection and your funky attitudes?

LERITA: I'll have to ponder that. It never occurred to me that they might be linked. I am certainly willing to do anything to move beyond the rejection episodes. I guess we need to stop now. I'm becoming fatigued.

GG: Yes, we'll talk again, Lerita. Thanks for listening.

LERITA: Sure.

Reflections

What emotion do you feel most of the time?

Can you identify any anger, disappointment or resentment you need to release?

Is there anyone you need to forgive?

How frequently do you feel joy, and what might foster more joy in your life?

Too Through
About six months after the transplant...

Sometimes I wonder if the heart transplant is a karmic debt I owe. What could I have done in some previous life that would warrant an experience like this? How many times do I have to be brought to the edge—to march, slide or be dragged through the Valley of the Shadow of Death? I know the route by heart now—I could walk it blindfolded.

Throughout this ordeal, my motto has been, "If I can't feel good, at least I ought to look good." Now with a prednisone induced moon face, not even my own family members recognize me. When my sister, Nicole first visited me in the hospital she came into my room and quickly left. My bloated body made her cry. I know it will go away eventually, but right now I feel ugly. So I try to maintain beautifully coiffed hair. My hairdresser, Barbara, who works in Denver, is my refuge, my holy sanctuary against all of the assaults on my body left by blood draws, biopsies, central lines, countless medications, and, of course, scars on my chest.

When I leave the beauty salon one Friday afternoon, I stop by the home of my dear friend Martha, who lives nearby, so I can make contact with her and her family. A real family lives in Martha's home—another anchor that I need in the months following the transplant. As a woman living alone, I want to experience community in my life. What a wonder to see four people sit down together and have dinner. How I miss my family and the dinner conversations of my childhood; sharing what's going on at school, whose game is coming up next, who needs new shoes, and what we are going to do after church on Sunday.

After walking into Martha's spotless kitchen, I plop down at the desk to call home and check voicemail. Scanning through the phone messages, it appears that Margaret Waller, the transplant coordinator, called to let me know that my biopsy results were back and I was "1A" and they want me to score zero.

I am beginning to feel like a medical doctor practicing without a license as I learn the intricacies and terminology of a transplant. Organ rejection is

134

measured by running a catheter down a vein in my neck (usually on the right side) through my tricuspid valve and into the heart to take small samples of heart tissue. These tissues are then examined under a microscope to determine if any rejection is occurring. In 1995, scores ranged from zero to four. I've seen "3A" more times than I would like, although they seem to be able to blast me back to a "2" pretty easily with some prednisone.

As I listen more closely, Margaret mentions that the transplant team wants me to start a new drug so my score will be consistently zero. My first response is an emphatic expletive. I am dizzy and feel woozy from what I am already taking. I told the doctors yesterday I am feeling ok, but not fine, and certainly not normal. *How could they consider giving me another, stronger immune-suppressing medication? It's called methotrexate. Isn't that some kind of abortion drug?* I want to cry, but there stands Martha ready to give me a tour of her sparkling and uncluttered house. I continue to hear Margaret's voice providing answers as thoughts swirl around in my head: *A strong drug?* "Just on the weekends," she said. *For how long?* "Five to eight weeks." *That sounds like September to me.* "We'll be watching you carefully. You won't need a biopsy for a while." *Side effects?* "Well…. this med could make you queasy, tired. Over time, maybe a little hair loss." I want to scream. *I want you all to get out of my life! You lied. You didn't tell me everything. Your funky little patient handbook didn't talk about ADVANCED REJECTION. I thought I would feel better after six to eight weeks. Now we're talking about six to nine months?*

I am working extremely hard at this transplant thing. It's by far the most difficult endeavor I've undertaken, more challenging than any job, school, or relationship I've ever experienced. I'm putting in more than 80 hours a week. Hell, this is harder than writing my dissertation or getting tenure. I'm getting tired—it seems like before I can recover from one thing my body is being zapped by the next.

Every time I have a rejection episode the doctors blast me with steroids. I am reeking with steroids. Besides the chipmunk face, my eyes water. As the hair on my head thins, thick black hair on my face spreads like wildfire. I looked in the mirror yesterday, called my brother and sobbed on the phone. When I pop in at church, most people don't approach because they don't recognize me. Last week one friend looked at me in disbelief and said, "Oh my God, Lerita. You look *so* different." Dating is clearly out of the question. Who is going to want a woman with my face and scars from incisions crisscrossing her chest like railroad tracks, in addition to the medical maintenance, pills, and doctor appointments?

I get the feeling that I am in a hallway and there are several doors. I know there is a light behind one of them. There is another one labeled "exit." I wonder if that is the one for me. That's the wild thing about the transplant journey. Once you're on this side, you are at the mercy of the doctors and God. You follow their program or you die. I don't think God wants me to die. Otherwise, I wouldn't be standing here in Martha's house with newly coiffed hair. I am so confused.

I pray, try to surrender, meditate; I scream for joy and in pain. My body is torn and worn down. What more must I do to keep this heart? Frustrated and depressed, I approach Grace with a proposition. I am quite surprised at her response.

LERITA: Grace, I've had it!

GG: Lerita, you sound very distressed, and you didn't say hello.

LERITA: Sorry about that. Hello.

GG: Gee, these funks you have are pretty bad, aren't they? What's wrong?

LERITA: I've had it, Grace. I'm sick of being sick. I'm tired of being hot. I'm tired of my ears ringing. I'm tired of being tired.

GG: I am very sorry, Lerita.

LERITA: Sorry won't get it this time. You haven't heard it all.

GG: There's more?

LERITA: I'm tired of doctors who don't listen, who don't answer the questions I ask, who don't have an answer but won't admit it. I'm tired of hearing "Well, we really don't know how these drugs work and they have different effects with different patients." That doesn't do a damn thing for my discomfort.

GG: I understand, but...

LERITA: Do you realize that I've been hot—every part of my body that touches anything is hot—since January?

GG: That's about six or seven months but...

LERITA: I've decided to end it.

GG: What?

LERITA: You heard me.

GG: What exactly do you mean, "end it," Lerita?

LERITA: Just what I said, "end it."

GG: As in die?

LERITA: Yes. It's over. I'm out of here.

GG: Why?

LERITA: (Sobbing) Why shouldn't I? What kind of life is this?

GG: Lerita. Are you ok?

LERITA: Obviously not. Look, Grace. Do you understand that I've been going to a doctor at least once a week for the past six months? I don't have a spouse, I don't even have a boyfriend and the prospects don't look good.

GG: Why do you think that?

LERITA: Look at me. I've got double bags around my eyes, my hair has thinned, there's the double chin and all sorts of odd additions to my muscle masses in the worst of places.

GG: Like where?

LERITA: Like my abdomen. Some people think I'm pregnant.

GG: Oh.

LERITA: And that would be an immaculate conception.

GG: Looks aren't everything, Lerita. Besides...

LERITA: Yeah, besides, who would want me?

GG: Perhaps someone who would search your heart and not solely focus on your physical appearance?

LERITA: I don't know anyone like that.

GG: You are in a deep funk today, huh?

LERITA: It's not only about men. I'm tired of the daily struggle. It is mentally and physically exhausting, and I don't see any easing soon.

GG: What is it that you are planning to do, Lerita?

LERITA: End it. Commit suicide.

GG: What? Why?

LERITA: I've just explained why. I'm sick of this.

GG: I understand that recovering from this transplant is very difficult, but what about me?

LERITA: What about you?

GG: You seemed to have forgotten that you did not go through this transplant alone. If you kill yourself, you kill me. I didn't go through all of this to be sentenced to death. What did I do wrong?

LERITA: What? What did you go through?

GG: How could you ask such a question? Who got cut out of another body, packed on ice and sewn into you? Now that's trauma. Who had to suffer through horribly high doses of anti-rejection drugs, and a body in chaotic confusion? Who's had to operate without being connected to a nervous system that regulates my beats? You talk about your body, but what about the changes to my shape?

LERITA: Grace, what are you talking about—your shape?

GG: The scar tissue from over 30 biopsies in the last six months. It's awful.

LERITA: If you say so. But Grace *I* am awfully tired.

GG: So am I, but have I given up? Have I ever stopped beating?

LERITA: No.

GG: Darn right. Did you know that hearts become exhausted? They tire of the physical, psychological and emotional abuse. Do you know how hard it is to pump through clogged up arteries? What about people who smoke and there's not enough oxygen in the blood? What about people who are angry or anxious or depressed all of the time? You think it is easy to pump under such conditions?

LERITA: I didn't think about that, Grace. What does that have to do with my case? I don't smoke, and I don't have clogged arteries.

GG: No, but you have enough funky emotions. I told you how badly it smells in here when things get emotionally loaded down. It makes me want to stop pumping. Although you are supposed to be recovering, you seem to be *doing* something all day. Talk about overworking me. And you haven't returned to work yet! Enough is enough. Despite all that we have been through together, the commitment we made to each other, I cannot believe you would jump ship. I get weary too, but I've never mentioned quitting. Besides, quite frankly, I am not ready to die.

LERITA: I've never thought about your side of it.

GG: I hate to say it but, Lerita, you're being very self-absorbed.

LERITA: I knew that was coming.

GG: I cannot help but remind you that the suffering is not all about you.

LERITA: I believe you've mentioned that I was selfish before.

GG: Lerita, did you notice that I said self-absorbed, not selfish. I think generally you are a very generous person, but you spend an awful lot of time focused on *you*, what *you* are thinking and feeling, or on what *you* want or need to do. Do you ever think about anybody else?

LERITA: You're hitting hard tonight. It doesn't sound like you, Grace.

GG: I have to. It's my existence too that you're considering ending. Like I said, I'm not ready to die.

LERITA: Why not?

GG: Because I want to see what else unfolds in your life? If it were supposed to be over, we would have died already. You had enough complications.

LERITA: Yes, Heavy assured me that I would not die having a transplant.

GG: And you want to kill yourself now?

LERITA: I am so miserable. I figure heaven has got to be better than this.

GG: What makes you think that? What makes you think that if you kill yourself, you're going to heaven?

LERITA: Don't give me that religious propaganda about going to hell if I commit suicide. I don't believe it.

GG: You know you're going to heaven?

LERITA: I think so. I've been a good person. I don't believe I deserve hell. Where else would I go?

GG: I'm not certain what your conception of an afterlife is, but I know if you kill yourself, I am turning into ash or I'm going to rot in the ground.

LERITA: It would be ash. I will definitely be cremated.

GG: Ash it is then. By the way, why are you being cremated?

LERITA: I'm deeply spiritual. I know the body is a container…

GG: For the spirit? Ok. Well if you're sure you're going to heaven, Lerita, just how do you plan to get there? You're certainly not going in a body. Bodies are either burned or they go into the ground. Bodies never leave the earth.

LERITA: I guess the same way I got here. This conversation is beginning to spook me out.

GG: Getting scared?

LERITA: Kind of.

GG: You're the one who wants to check out. Where are you going and how are you going to get there?

LERITA: Like I said, I'm going to heaven.

GG: What is your fantasy of heaven?

LERITA: I've heard that the streets are paved with gold.

GG: So, without a body, you're going to need a street?

LERITA: Ok. I dunno, I get another body?

GG: You think if you die you can escape this "horrible experience" here, as you describe it. But you are afraid to die, aren't you, Lerita?

LERITA: Yes.

GG: Isn't that a contradiction?

LERITA: Yes, but I don't know what else to do.

GG: Are you sure if you commit suicide, you're going to someplace better than this?

LERITA: What do you mean?

GG: Most people who choose to die, to kill themselves, believe they will escape to a better place but what about *this* world?

LERITA: I'm lost, Grace.

GG: Lerita, trust me. Your state of mind is vital.

LERITA: What does my mind have to do with it?

GG: It creates what you see.

LERITA: I still don't get it.

GG: Hear me out. If you think life is hell, it is. If you want to see heaven, you will. Wherever you are, you take your state of mind. Remember that phrase from the Bible, "As a man thinketh in his heart so is he?"

LERITA: Yes.

GG: It's true. If you are angry, bitter, frustrated or disappointed about everything, that is the kind of experience you will have here.

LERITA: It wouldn't be better to leave for heaven?

GG: Right now, if heaven appeared right in front of you, you wouldn't be able to enjoy it—do you understand?

LERITA: I think so

GG: Ever heard the phrase: "I'm in heaven" or "This is heavenly?"

LERITA: Yes.

GG: How are you *feeling* at the time?

LERITA: Absolutely wonderful. Oh, I get it. I could experience a taste of heaven right here on earth if I felt wonderful.

GG: "Blessed are the pure in heart, for they shall see God." You can see God in everything and everybody when your heart is not burdened down with anger, resentment, depression, self-pity or thoughts of suicide, when your heart is clean.

LERITA: Yes, but where is the heaven in all of the suffering I'm doing right now with this transplant?

GG: It all has to do with focus, Lerita.

LERITA: Focus?

GG: Yes. Look at what you focus on. You don't like the doctors. The medication makes you feel queasy. The recovery is taking too long. Is there anything going right?

LERITA: I guess I *am* concentrating on the negative aspects.

GG: Have you forgotten the basic things like amazing health insurance, a beautiful home and car? You will have a job to return to after you recover. You have wonderful friends and family who are present to support you. Didn't one of your cousins ride the train all the way from Detroit to stay with you for a week? Have you eaten since you returned from the hospital? Who's cooking the food, washing the clothes, and cleaning the house?

LERITA: I haven't thought about *those* things, about how I feel loved.

GG: If you would focus on the love and not the suffering and let go of some of that anger and impatience you have about the transplant, you may find in the end that you are being transformed and the transplant was the best thing that ever happened to you.

LERITA: I am definitely not there. I have a lot of work to do.

GG: I think you need to sit with this for a while. But I have another question for you, Lerita.

LERITA: What is that?

GG: What would you teach by killing yourself?

LERITA: I'm not teaching any courses right now. I am home recovering.

GG: Life is the classroom. Every person teaches something—love, courage, hate, fear. You're always teaching.

LERITA: That is the last thing I want to hear!

GG: Do you want to model, "When the going gets tough, the tough give up?"

LERITA: No, not really.

GG: Think about all of the people who become ill every year, all of the people who face trauma and life crises. They may lose their home or a job; lose a loved one or a limb. Possibly, an accident leaves them a quadriplegic, or it's cancer of some kind. Do you want to teach them to give up, to commit suicide?

LERITA: WHAT DO I NEED TO TEACH, GRACE?

GG: You are raising your voice, Lerita. It's only you and me here. How about teaching others to hold some faith and hope in their hearts. You've got to trust that "this too will pass." A little trust and a heart full of hope can go a long way.

LERITA: Was that a pun?

GG: Not from me. "Heart full" is a manner of speech, and when properly used it can convey...

LERITA: I got it, Grace. I was trying to get you to lighten up.

GG: You've got my demise and yours on the line here, Lerita. This is no time for humor.

LERITA: Wouldn't a little laughter make us both feel better?

GG: My joy springs from a deeper space than that produced by laughter associated with jokes. I don't generate funks and feelings that interfere with natural joy, you do. Unfortunately, I have to hold the happy and the sad, the anger and the anxiety for you. Natural joy is so much better than any of the feelings you generate with false laughter.

LERITA: Preach on, Rev. Grace. I would agree. It is an inherently different feeling. But that kind of joy is rare and fleeting.

GG: It's more natural than you think. However, don't you think we've talked enough? It's been a long, draining day.

LERITA: Yeah. I'm getting tired.

GG: You can say that again.

LERITA: Yeah. I'm getting tired...

GG: We can also talk later about *your* sense of humor. Are you sure you are okay? You don't need to call someone to help you sort this out?

LERITA: Actually, you've done a great job, Grace. Thanks so much.

GG: Please promise me—no more talk about killing us.

LERITA: I promise.

GG: Thanks, Lerita. Talk with you later.

LERITA: OK.

Reflections

Have you ever felt so hopeless about a situation that you wanted to escape?

What role does the adage, "No matter where you go, there you are" play in your life experiences?

What beliefs do you hold about an afterlife and where do they come from?

What about God?
About eight months after the transplant...

The moment the beeper went off in the early morning of January 9th, my life changed forever. At the time I was on my personal quest to become a celebrity in the field of social psychology. My friend, Julian, called such people "minor celebrities" because so few people outside of their own discipline actually knew who they were. Still, in the academic world, it seemed important. My colleagues spent so much time and energy jockeying for position in our little pond and I felt compelled to jump right in.

At a young age I developed the notion that I was born to do something exceptional, be someone special or famous, so I set out to make it happen. I'm not sure when such thoughts started floating through and lodging in a special cranny in my mind, but the dreams grew bigger and the stakes higher. In high school, I yearned to be selected one of the "Lucky 13" top students in the senior class, and I was. In college, I needed to graduate with "college honors" and "highest honors in the major," and I did.

As I began my academic career, I desired to win a Nobel Prize even though they don't award one in psychology. I was like the young person who, when asked "What do you want to be?" replies, "I want to be famous" or "I want to be a movie star" instead of wanting to become an actor or someone who loves theatre or the dramatic arts. It is not that I disliked psychology and the academy—I truly loved to teach students, to awaken them from an often long, intellectually deprived slumber. But I am driven. I want to be known, recognized, admired, and respected for my contributions to the field of psychology. I need to be extraordinary and memorable in psychology like Sigmund Freud, Carl Jung or Mamie and Kenneth Clark.

The heart transplant changed everything. How can I look deeply into the eyes of death and remain the same? I can no longer afford to be ambitious, anxious, controlling, and a perfectionist striving to be number one. In part, I don't have the physical or emotional stamina to sustain such insanity. Quite simply, I don't want that kind of life anymore. I don't want the kind of pseudo-happiness that is contingent upon crossing off everything on a daily list, publishing another article, or securing a large research grant. I don't want my gratification to depend on living in the right neighborhood, being on the "A" list for social events, or driving the latest model of the most prestigious car. What I truly yearn for is peace and joy. I want to awaken happy in the mornings. I want to be content because I exist and for me to enter that state, a major transformation is imperative. I need another purpose for my life.

Living a balanced life, especially with a heart transplant, is tough. I'm not talking about activity versus rest, although despite Heavy Harvey's admonition, I still try to fit more events into a day than are humanly possible. I refuse to acknowledge that my recovery is going to take longer than nine months. I aggressively pursue or orchestrate whatever I want. Could that be why Heavy Harvey manifested as a heart with a *"masculine tone?"* When is my nurturing, self-compassionate side allowed to express itself, even in my own self-care?

The wisdom of both of my hearts is phenomenal. It is a knowingness that I never chose to access because I had the plan all mapped out. I seem to be emerging from a deep sleep. It is time to cultivate a new self, or develop some parts of myself that I've permitted to lie dormant. Perhaps I can allow my authentic self to materialize rather than constantly feed my driven and compulsive false self. If nothing else, I need to clear away the debris that keeps me from beginning anew. I work to maintain the same trust in God or a Higher Power that I summoned when they wheeled me into the OR. I have to go with the flow and let go of everything—slights, disappointments, hopelessness, and self-criticism.

So many questions flow from these realizations. *What gives me joy? Who and what do I need to change my mind about?* Letting go of some of the learned, automatic responses is a scary proposition, but that's where my faith and trust in my Creator must lead me. Even though I may be afraid of an intimate relationship with God, I cannot run away from this deeper awareness, nor can I sidestep it to do my own thing anymore. How many times must I be saved from some awful calamity? Will I ever believe that God loves me and that I deserve this life-sparing transplant? This is my true grace period, and I need help from both of my hearts to facilitate my own extreme makeover.

GG: Hey Lerita?

LERITA: Are you calling me, Grace?

GG: Yes, I am. Are you ready to finish our last conversation?

LERITA: We weren't done? Thanks for providing me with a different perspective. Now that I've had time to consider your insights, I see that the thoughts of suicide were a bit extreme. But I am still unsure how to get out of "hell."

GG: As I was saying before, paying attention to what you focus on is essential to your recovery.

LERITA: How can I *not* focus on my transplant? It's a way life is now.

GG: That's what you *think*. The heart transplant is not your whole life, Lerita. You had another life before it happened.

LERITA: Yes. Actually, I was involved in several activities but....

GG: You've stopped thinking about and doing them. You need to get back to some of your pre-transplant life.

LERITA: I am beginning to do that. The academic year begins soon.

GG: That's great. Otherwise, you have three choices. First, you can continue to wallow in the "woe is me."

LERITA: Oh yeah, Heavy told me about the pity-party for one.

GG: Good, then you are familiar with the idea.

LERITA: Ok.

GG: Second, you can be grateful for this wondrous time in your life. We talked about that in the last conversation. Look at how much better you are doing now than last year at this time.

LERITA: Oh?

GG: Before the transplant weren't you going rapidly downhill toward death by being in and out of heart failure? Weren't you taking blood thinners and medicines to keep your heart pumping?

LERITA: (Sighing) Yeah.

GG: How could you forget that?

LERITA: You're right, and I could hardly get out of bed. I am still not feeling as well as I did before the transplant—before I became extremely ill. I want to feel better.

GG: Do you know how many people die waiting for an organ? You got me in four days!

LERITA: It was a miracle.

GG: And you got me, Grace.

LERITA: Getting a little narcissistic on me?

GG: Don't you think I'm the perfect heart for you? I'm not Heavy Harvey, but you must admit we're a great match.

LERITA: Yes, I guess so.

GG: Could you be a little more enthusiastic? No, I don't have Heavy's wit and heart-pun humor, but I suspect I am more at peace than he was. I certainly didn't come with his load. Look what you heaped on him all of those years. Jody may have felt conflicted, but she engaged in a lot of inner reflection as her 40th birthday approached. You know, Lerita, your inner life is where the action is. That is where the healing occurs. I think you call it self-reflection. A lot of Jody's heart space was clear.

LERITA: You're wonderful, Grace. But you're not Heavy. I still miss him.

GG: You're definitely not my Jody. I miss her too, but you're not so bad. You have a few rough edges, but basically, you are a good person.

LERITA: I can't believe this—analysis by my heart!

GG: Yes, and it is the best kind. Hearts will tell you the truth.

LERITA: You're right.

GG: Like we talked about last time, you've got to keep the heart space clear. You can't let those funky feelings build up, clog up and suffocate your heart. Besides, you won't be able to hear G.O.D.

LERITA: G.O.D.?

GG: You know the book, *The Artist's Way,* the one you are reading now? The authors talk about G.O.D. or Good Orderly Direction. I wish Jody had read that book. She had lots of talents she was interested in developing.

LERITA: Really. I took a class on it.

GG: That brings me to the third choice, Lerita.

LERITA: What is that?

GG: You can focus on the still place.

LERITA: The still place? Where?

GG: In your mind.

LERITA: Is that what some people refer to as the quiet spot? Where is that? There's chatter in my mind all of the time.

GG: Yes. I know you have a very active mind, Lerita. However, there is a quiet, still place inside of it.

LERITA: Does this have anything to do with the little Voice? Heavy talked about listening to a little Voice.

GG: That's the Good Orderly Direction I am speaking of, Lerita. If you pause more often and be still, you can feel a Presence, or as you refer to it, "Spirit" communicating. It's your spiritual heart that lies deep within me. You cannot hear that Voice if you are burdened by racing thoughts and negative feelings.

LERITA: Does everyone have a quiet spot?

GG: Yes, everyone does. But unless each person pauses to quiet the mind and heart on occasion, a rarity I might add for you, they may never be aware of the Guidance.

LERITA: Thanks a lot.

GG: It's not a criticism, Lerita, it's merely an observation. There's a difference you know. You're normal. Usually, you have the radio or television blasting, or you've got some fantasy conversation playing out in your mind either about something you should have said in the past or how you're going to handle so-and-so in the future. You make an attempt to be quiet when you sit in silence, but normally you're chattering away.

LERITA: You can hear these conversations?

GG: Hearts hear, feel, and hold *everything*.

LERITA: How is this so-called still spot going to get me out of the hell I'm in right now?

GG: When you focus on the stillness within you, you create more space in your heart to hear the Voice, the Guidance. It usually doesn't communicate in words, although in circumstances of imminent danger or for urgent messages, you might hear a direct audible command. It's more like urges.

LERITA: Like the intuition that Heavy Harvey spoke about?

GG: Yes.

LERITA: The Spirit communicates through the "little Voice"?

GG: Yes, yes. The Spirit will guide you out of the hell you find yourself in if you listen attentively. Taking one day at a time or one moment at a time and taking time for solitude will help tremendously.

LERITA: All I need to do is be still and listen?

GG: Yes, but it isn't easy. In the stillness, you begin to know when and where to go. You may need to talk about why you think life is hell with your therapist or a spiritual director, or you may need to take some anti-depressive or anti-anxiety medications. You might need to join a support group. I am certain there are many patients who face similar challenges, and they might have great insights to offer. Or maybe you need to read a certain book or call your sister. The guidance is not always the same, and it varies depending on the situation. You suffer needlessly because the answers you receive to your prayers and requests are frequently not in a form you like or they don't fit your expectations.

LERITA: I can relate to that. I prayed for a miraculous healing from my heart disease. Instead, I got a heart transplant.

GG: Lerita, don't you see? A heart transplant *is* a miraculous healing.

LERITA: I meant *a healing* where I wasn't forced to have surgery, pain, strong drugs, biopsies...

GG: Lerita. Look at all of the healing you *are* doing, especially the spiritual healing. Look at how Heavy Harvey helped to clear your heart space so there would be room for me to sing and dance.

LERITA: Yes.

GG: You needed some release from those emotions to be healed. They were loading you down, holding you back. If you had experienced miraculous healing in the form you wanted, you'd still be carrying that load. And the stench would have put me out of commission long ago. That is why this path was chosen for your healing. Don't you feel lighter than you did before?

LERITA: I do and because I received you, Grace.

GG: I care for you now that we've been together for several months. I've grown fond of you, and I am genuinely happy that I am in your life. I think we need to stay together. The best is yet to come.

LERITA: Gosh, I am touched, Grace. I wasn't sure how this new heart thing would work. I couldn't imagine letting Heavy go, no matter how sick he was. But I like you. You have a kind, gentle, sweetness about you. I am happy that I got you. I'll try to hang in there.

GG: Then, let's get some rest.

LERITA: Great idea, Grace. Thanks so much for the wisdom.

GG: You are welcome

Reflections

How might you describe your inner life?

Do you pay attention to your thoughts and how they affect your outlook, emotions, and behavior?

Have you heard guidance or Good Orderly Direction (G.O.D.) while being quiet or in sitting in a quiet location? What was your response?

Definitely Not Sleepless in Boulder
About ten months after the transplant...

As I return to teaching, I begin to notice some of the things that Heavy Harvey mentioned. Despite the trauma of a transplant, I am still driven. Why can't I feel comfortable being a "regular person" as Dr. Martinez, my therapist, describes it? Where is this need for so much external applause coming from? I could blame Mom and Dad for my high need for approval, but how long can I hold them responsible for everything?

Last year on a river-rafting trip, I learned that it's ok to coast sometimes. I don't need to paddle rapidly for the entire journey. In fact, I shouldn't. Life is a marathon, not a sprint. I cannot remain this ambitious and expect to live, especially now that I am on my second heart. I've got to slow down. How do I slow down in a world that is moving faster than I can think? I could generate some internal applause by celebrating myself—rejoicing about my survival of this transplant as well as my new willingness to stop and rest. I will take my hearts' advice and cut the daily to-do list and schedule in half.

Grace is amazingly wise, and she offers such helpful insights. Like Heavy, she encourages me to change the perceptions I hold about my life and myself. Yet I still struggle with the medical regimen and working full-time. I am habitually fatigued, mentally and physically. Keeping up with classes, research, writing, the house, doctor's appointments, medications, and medical procedures tests my ingenuity.

Yesterday, while lecturing to a group of graduate students, I forgot what I wanted to say. I stood there petrified in front of ten curious and attentive faces seated around the table in the seminar room. Lapses of memory of this sort never happened to me before the transplant, so I kept talking until I found my way back to the point. Serious thinking now feels like I am wandering through a densely populated forest, hoping that I will find my way out. With no guide and the uncharted territory of my mind on a multitude of anti-rejection drugs and anti-hypertensive medications, I struggle to keep my thoughts in logical order.

In the midst of this transition to work, Grace and I don't speak. When do I have time? Then an intriguing-looking letter arrives in the mail. I don't recognize the handwriting or the return address. I am grateful it is not a bill or notice from an insurance company. I wonder who would write me from Denver instead of calling. After I put down my briefcase and files, I slowly open the lovely stationery with earth tones of orange and green that matches the autumn leaves falling outside. Given the stationery and handwriting, I suspect the sender is a woman. I begin to read the letter: *"Dear Lerita, I have waited a long time for this day. I have wanted to meet you ever since my dear friend Jody passed away last January…"* I look at the signature: *Cathy Brase.* This letter is from Jody's best friend. Cathy and I had given permission to Donor Alliance about a month ago to exchange personal information and to meet in person. I'm not sure if I am ready. I know it is time to contact Grace for some counsel, but I choose to wait until the next morning.

LERITA: Grace?

GG: (no answer)

LERITA: Oh Grace?

GG: (no answer)

LERITA: Grace, why aren't you answering? I know you are there.

GG: Oh, uh, hi. I was having such a nice sleep.

LERITA: Did I wake you? I'm sorry. Wait a minute. Sleep? How could you be sleeping? Hearts aren't supposed to sleep!

GG: (Yawning) It's a figure of speech. Let's just say we go into another state of consciousness.

LERITA: Another state of consciousness?! What are you talking about?

GG: Lerita, you're very melodramatic, huh?

LERITA: You're calling me melodramatic, and you're talking about sleeping?

GG: It would be very helpful to both of us if you calmed down. Are you ok?

LERITA: Yeah, sure, but Heavy Harvey told me that hearts beat all of the time. They never sleep on the job.

GG: Heavy was right. I didn't say I had *stopped* beating. I was resting. Haven't you noticed that your heart rate is slower when you are sleeping or resting?

LERITA: Yes, it is much slower in the mornings when I first wake up.

GG: That's what I mean. We rest when you rest, but we never stop beating. Like I said, I was resting. What time is it anyway?

LERITA: About 5:30.

GG: A.M.?

LERITA: Now look who's getting excited. I thought you and Jody were morning people.

GG: Oh no! Jody was not a morning person. In fact, she always selected the afternoon and evening shifts at work. And she loved to sleep in. It was sooo wonderful.

LERITA: Then she was the laid back kind?

GG: Not at all. In fact, many times she pushed the limits. There was a part of her that was very driven. She kept her retail sales high. But she loved to sleep.

LERITA: (Mumbling softly) Driven like me?

GG: I didn't mean anything about you.

LERITA: How can I ever get anything done if I am sleeping in?

GG: We can talk about slowing down and relaxing later. You obviously contacted me to talk about something else.

LERITA: It wasn't important. Are you up to talking or should I wait until noon?

GG: I can talk but will you promise me that we will take a nap later this afternoon?

LERITA: I can't believe I have a heart that likes to sleep.

GG: That's *rest*. I don't mind resting. You lead a pretty active life, Lerita. With teaching, tailoring lessons, book clubs, cooking. I can't see where you relax.

LERITA: Sewing is relaxing.

GG: Yes, but it takes concentration and mental activity. When you are thinking, you are not relaxing and neither am I. Do you ever do nothing or sit around and veg—you know, like lay out on a nice day and watch the clouds float across the sky?

LERITA: Sometimes, but it's not my style. I like to keep busy.

GG: I see. What was it that you wanted to talk about?

LERITA: Oh yeah. I want to call Cathy, Jody's friend. I received a letter some time ago from Donor Alliance, but I thought it might be too early for a meeting. Then last month I sent a request for information exchange, and I received a letter yesterday with an address and telephone number for her. I am still not sure if I should contact her.

GG: That's great. Cathy is such a wonderful person. Did I mention that she and Jody were best friends for over 11 years?

LERITA: You know her?

GG: Of course. Hearts know all of the people you are connected to. Thinking about Cathy brings back fond memories. She and Jody were like sisters. Remember Jody was the only girl in her family. When her Mom passed away, she felt lost and lonely, especially when her Dad remarried a year or so later. Jody and Cathy shopped, hiked, and hung out together.

LERITA: I want to call her, but I don't know what to say.

GG: How about "Hello?"

LERITA: Are you being sarcastic?

GG: No I'm not. Cathy isn't difficult to talk to. She's very nice.

LERITA: I am having so much trouble knowing what to do. I continue to celebrate life, but Jody's family and friends must still be grieving. I suspect the first year after the loss of a loved one is the hardest.

GG: I understand. You feel guilty for being happy that you are doing so well because Jody is gone.

LERITA: Yes. I guess I have been avoiding or denying it. I feel like I have some responsibility to lead a better life since someone died in order for me to have a new heart, to have you.

GG: That's a heavy burden of guilt you're putting on both of us, Lerita. Jody was going to die. I'm sure you will be grateful forever to her family for agreeing to donate me to you, but does it mean that you have to be a better person?

LERITA: It seems that way to me.

GG: Isn't illness an opportunity to change your life or simplify things rather than add to the stress?

LERITA: Oh, definitely. Actually, despite my busy schedule, I *have* slowed down. I used to feed my ego. Now I feel much better when I share my love for books or cooking or sewing with others. I've lost the inclination to impress people. I feel passionate about sewing, reading, cinema, and theatre and I want to pass on the joy.

GG: That's a great attitude and very good for the heart.

LERITA: Thanks. I look at people differently. I finally understand that everyone who comes to the earth is here to heal, everyone. A homeless person, a king, or a wall street broker—we are all spiritual beings who are finding our way back home to God. I hold more compassion for people, no matter who they are. Everyone is trying to figure it out, some with greater difficulty than others. I wonder why that is the case?

GG: Egos are so alluring. They make you think that if you obtain certain items, you will be happy. If you buy another house, or acquire another job with a more prestigious title, or marry another spouse, you'll be happy. None of these can make you happy, because happiness is about having a happy heart. If you are not happy in your heart, nothing else matters.

LERITA: So, happiness and joy come from having a happy heart?

GG: That's right. We've talked about this before.

LERITA: Yes, we have, but that's a huge lesson.

GG: Eventually everyone will get it, but it may take a long time for some.

LERITA: That's too bad. It seems like such needless suffering.

GG: It is. It's because each human spirit possesses volition. You can always choose how you feel and what you do. At the same time, because of your heart, you can always *know* how you feel. If you don't feel peace and joy, then you're not connecting with your deeper spiritual heart. You are letting other feelings get in the way. For some people, sooner or later they will get tired of being unhappy, and the light bulb will come on. Others are more obstinate and refuse to pay attention, so they suffer more.

LERITA: I am familiar with that form of suffering. Heavy Harvey reminded me of how stubborn I can be. Hopefully, I'm going to stay on the path of peace and joy this time.

GG: You seem to be doing pretty well these days. I haven't felt any major build-up of anger, disappointment or depression lately. Your heart-space is clear. It gives me lots of room to sing and dance. I guess the previous conversations helped.

LERITA: I keep imagining a singing and dancing heart. What a sight!

GG: Absolutely. Unfortunately, most hearts are weighed down with so much baggage that we just stop—beating, that is.

LERITA: Is that what happens with a heart attack?

GG: Somewhat. Diet and exercise are important too, but when people are burdened, they don't take time to eat properly or exercise, especially people who are worried or depressed. It's more complicated, but mood, diet, and exercise are linked. Uh, Lerita, do you mind if we go back to sleep now?

LERITA: Sleep? You really like your sleep!

GG: Five a.m. is a little early for me. How about a couple more hours of sleep?

LERITA: What about Cathy? What should I do about calling Cathy?

GG: (No answer)

LERITA: Grace?

GG: (No answer)

LERITA: (Softly) Oh, Grace

GG: (No answer)

LERITA: GRACE!

GG: Oh my God, please don't take me out again! I promise I won't bother anybody! Help me!

LERITA: Grace. It's okay. I guess I must have awakened you. Did you fall asleep while I was talking to you?

GG: Oh it's you. God, I thought I was having a nightmare. It seemed they were trying to cut me out again.

LERITA: I am sorry to frighten you. Sounds like you need your sleep. I mean rest.

GG: Lerita, I would love to talk, but don't you think it is a little early for these serious heart-to-heart conversations?

LERITA: A heart pun. It reminds me of Harvey. He liked...

GG: (Softly) ... those heart puns. What did you want to ask me before I started resting?

LERITA: Oh yeah. I asked you about calling Cathy. I am afraid to call her.

GG: Call her. She'll be happy to hear from you. She's written you two letters hasn't she?

LERITA: Yes, and I want to meet her, but I don't know if I can face her pain.

GG: Trust me. Your call will ease her pain. I know she is happy that some part of Jody lives on in you, in us.

LERITA: (Smiling) Thanks. Two more hours of sleep, huh? That's a lot.

GG: Pleasant dreams?

LERITA: Ok. I relent. Pleasant dreams.

Reflections

Have you ever experienced bittersweet moments when something went well for you but not for someone else?

What do you feel passionate about? Do you share your passions with others?

Have you felt the peace and joy that lies deep within your heart? If not, what do you think is blocking it?

Do you give your body, especially your heart, enough rest? If not, why not?

The Holidays with a New Heart
About eleven months after the transplant...

As Grace and I approach our first Christmas together, I reflect back to last Christmas. Unbeknownst to me, on Christmas day, 1994, I was approximately two weeks from a heart transplant. I had plenty to write in my journal that Christmas morning.

It was my choice. The family yielded to my request to have Christmas at my brother Kenneth's home in Oakland, California. I am back in the Bay Area, a place I often travel to for solace, comfort, and recuperation. Fog in the morning; shimmering lights in the evening... I love to look out over San Francisco Bay and feel its soothing and calming effects. It reminds me of the balm the beautiful Rocky Mountains offer. In the stillness of this Christmas morning, I want to capture in my journal the mishmash of thoughts and feelings occurring in my mind and heart. For the first time, I have an opportunity to see Christmas in a different light.

Huddled before the tall, snow-flocked Christmas tree with all the glittering lights and dancing ornaments, the thoughts come quickly. Here I sit alone, while everyone else sleeps. I cannot believe all I have been through in the last few months. Unexpected visits to the hospital with congestive heart failure, immobilizing exhaustion, fears about falling asleep and not waking up. I wasn't certain if I would see this Christmas, and I wonder if this is my last Christmas with Mom, Dad, Kenneth, Robert, and Nicole.

Usually, I am ambivalent about Christmas. I feel a festive joy that is clouded by depression and resentment. I keep anticipating that each new holiday season will be different, like the Christmases in the storybooks or on the television specials where the family decorates the tree together, sings Christmas carols, laughs about old times and truly enjoys the beauty of being connected to each other. It never seems that way in our house. I wonder if that sense of joyous communion exists in anyone's house, or if all of that holiday cheer is another fabrication of modern media and wishful thinking. By the end of Christmas Day, I usually feel tense, tired, and glad it will be another year before I go through the motions again. In fact, I've often remarked that I would be fine if Christmas occurred only once every five years.

Historically, I spend Christmas time being the dutiful daughter. I help purchase and decorate the tree, bake cookies and cakes, and along with Mom, organize and cook most of Christmas breakfast and dinner. Wrapping gifts is one of my favorite holiday activities, but often I feel like an unfilled box wrapped with beautiful paper. Especially at Christmas, I act loving toward my family, but deep down inside I feel angry and resentful. In my observations, Mom and I work hard while others sit around and consume what we prepare. I wonder when the rest of the family is going to join this production. Despite my outward appearance of goodwill and sweetness, thoughts of bitterness and spite confine me to an earthly hell.

Why does Christmas seem nicer this year? Is it the ominous heart transplant looming? Death is staring me in the face. Just in case I don't make it, I ask the Holy Spirit to help me this Christmas. I ask for help with forgiveness; for some release of all of the resentment I'm carrying in my heart. If this is possibly my last Christmas, I want to have a different feeling about the season and the people I've shared it with for so many years.

I sense this health crisis offers me another perspective, some perceptual and spiritual insights. My recent soul searching shifts my focus. I observe how each family member works to make this Christmas a happy one instead of being centered on what they are not doing.

Remarkably, Kenneth bought the Christmas tree, and he, Dad, and Robert decorated it while Mom, Nicole and Kenneth's girlfriend, Valerie, and I looked on. We sang Christmas carols last night like on television. We laughed, and we cried. What a change! Why does it take a crisis for people to realize that they love each other? Do we need the threat of death for us to treat each other with affection and kindness?

As I relinquish my animosity, I feel the peace and joy that lie beneath it in my heart. Every year, Christmas seemed like such a burden, but now I believe it is a once-a-year opportunity to see others, and myself, in a different way. It is about the renewal of love, a subtle and sometimes not-so-subtle reminder of my connection to my family and friends, a bond my lack of forgiveness frequently severs. This Christmas I receive the best gift ever—a totally new vision.

That was last year. What is this Christmas with a new heart going to be like? I miss Heavy Harvey, and I sense that Grace misses Jody. The feeling of loss is in the air. Hopefully, we can cheer each other up during this holiday season.

GG: Lorita, Lorita, Lorita

LERITA: (no answer)

GG: Oh, Lorita.

LERITA: Grace, it's pronounced Loo-rita.

GG: Sorry.

LERITA: Are you all right? You sound awfully excited.

GG: Oh, I am. It was fantastic, all of the music, singing and clapping. I wanted to shout. I wanted to scream. I felt like doing a jig.

LERITA: Doing a jig?

GG: Yes, dancing—doing a jig.

LERITA: But a jig? Why a jig?

GG: Isn't that what you do when you're happy? Don't you want to do a jig?

LERITA: Jig is not exactly the word I would use, but I understand what you mean. It must be a cultural difference.

GG: Hmm. Quite possibly. I've never heard music and singing like that.

LERITA: You've never been to a gospel concert?

GG: I guess not. Is that what you call it?

LERITA: Yes. It's an African-American tradition. Nice isn't it?

GG: Oh yes. It's so uplifting. That kind of singing makes me want to dance. I … you …we were kind of dragging before the concert, but afterward, I felt like I could do anything, that I could live forever.

LERITA: I know the feeling. I was, or we were, exhausted before the concert. What was that about?

GG: You were so busy with packing, grading papers, and purchasing Christmas gifts before you left that we almost ran out of energy. Then there was the plane trip.

LERITA: Yeah, that was something else wasn't it?

GG: The dip the plane took during that bout of turbulence was rough. I was sure we were going down.

LERITA: It scared me too. I thought you were going to drop to my feet. There were people screaming, and food was flying.

GG: I'm sewn in pretty tight, Lerita. I don't think I'll be falling out of your chest.

LERITA: The thought passed through my mind a few times.

GG: I understand, but seriously, I can't see how I could ever come undone.

LERITA: I knew we wouldn't crash, though. There was no way, after 11 months and all of the crap we've been through, that we would end our life together in an airplane crash.

GG: I agree. I don't think it's our time yet and especially on a flight from Denver to LA.

LERITA: I still feel a bit of sadness. I can't figure it out.

GG: Oh, that was me.

LERITA: You? What do you have to be sad about? I thought everything was getting better, fewer drugs, less side effects, more energy.

GG: All of that is wonderful. Super. I guess it's the holidays—Christmas and all.

LERITA: Isn't Christmas supposed to be a joyous time? You're always talking to me about making space for singing and dancing.

GG: Having a clear heart space is very important—vital to being alive. But something is missing.

LERITA: What is it then?

GG: It's Jody.

LERITA: You miss her, huh?

GG: She was always so excited about the holidays. There was the dazzling tree, the gorgeous gifts. With Jody working retail, it was a busy time of year for her. Frequently she spent the holidays with her Dad and her brothers. She liked being part of a family.

LERITA: Jody felt the Christmas spirit?

GG: Yes. It's so heart-warming. Oh, I didn't mean to make a pun.

LERITA: It's ok. I understand. Some people get into full swing during Christmas. They love to create those warm, fuzzy feelings of the holiday season.

GG: Jody liked to bake cookies and cakes. There was this yummy cranberry walnut bread with...

LERITA: I typically bake cookies too. But since I was going to spend Christmas in California, I decided I would only bake a cake.

GG: Is that why you didn't put up any Christmas decorations?

LERITA: Yes, because I was leaving. Remember, my plans for Christmas in California?

GG: You don't decorate your own house every year?

LERITA: I don't see the point when I am so busy, and I won't be around for Christmas. I both love and hate Christmas, and I am still trying to cope with my ambivalence. I want to have some balance in my life. I cannot do everything.

GG: What did you do last year?

LERITA: Due to the looming heart transplant, I worked hard to have a special Christmas with my family at my brother's house in the Bay Area. Because Heavy was failing, the physical exhaustion curtailed my baking. Besides, I don't think most people have the spirit. They give out of habit.

GG: Some may.

LERITA: I think there are lots of people who try to create that happy holiday atmosphere, but it doesn't work for me. I spend a lot of time and energy running around, and I don't feel a special connection.

GG: Have you considered that you are centered on the wrong things.

LERITA: Actually, I came to that realization last Christmas.

GG: Lots of people have been brainwashed, Lerita.

LERITA: How so?

GG: You've been kidnapped by the commercialization of Christmas. Remember the first Christmas, and many that followed weren't like that.

LERITA: It's true. There's so much emphasis on gifts. I love to wrap them, but there never seems to be enough time to engage in my favorite holiday activities. I like to write Christmas cards and reach out to old friends or family I haven't seen or heard from in years. I want to feel a connection.

GG: Have you noticed that people yearn for connection and run from it at the same time? You have to let things be. Quit running around at Christmas trying to find the perfect gifts. It's the love behind the gift that fuels the connection, the true feeling of warmth that the Christmas season brings.

LERITA: I understand, Grace, but love is very complicated. People in my family expect nice gifts, and I think many people equate love with expensive gifts.

GG: Like I said, they are brainwashed by the commercialism.

LERITA: I want my family and friends to know that I am thinking of them but we're too old and have far too much junk already to be exchanging extravagant gifts.

GG: Think about what your intention is with the gift, Lerita. What do you want to convey?

LERITA: I want them to know that I love and care for them. I see what you are saying, Grace. Love doesn't mean big and impressive.

GG: Let the intention, the desire to connect in a special way, guide the little Christmas shopping you feel absolutely compelled to do. By the way, what would be the perfect Christmas for you, Lerita?

LERITA: Great question! My perfect Christmas would involve getting together with family and friends for a series of small gatherings or meals over two or three days. Christmas Eve, Christmas Day and the day after Christmas are great times when people feel a loss. Of course, there would be lots of breaks and time for people to exhale, relax, take a nap, listen to music or watch movies. We could exchange trinkets or small gifts that remind us of some good memory or childhood.

GG: You could make each other food. How about fixing each other's favorite dish or you each fix a special part of the meal?

LERITA: It's a nice dream, Grace. What if I'm not feeling love?

GG: Then you need to search your heart to find out what is blocking the love. Try to release whatever is in the way and ask for help in letting it go.

LERITA: I guess I am still trying to do too much.

GG: Can you eliminate anything? How about making it simple? One cake is all the family needs.

LERITA: Simple. That could be challenging, but I am willing to try.

GG: You want to feel the authentic spirit of Christmas, instead of the one the advertisers created, right?

LERITA: Yes.

GG: You're no different from anyone else. Everyone wants to feel connected to someone. That's why it's not the presents, the diamond ring, the new car or the new suit. If what you receive isn't given with love, then the feeling of love is missing too. With stuff alone, you feel empty, especially after Christmas is over.

LERITA: Is that why I am depressed the day after Christmas?

GG: Could be. Remember, Lerita, Christmas can be every day. Each time you break down some barrier; each time you manage to connect with someone, you experience what we all want to feel at Christmas.

LERITA: Christmas was great last year when everyone in the family participated and loved being together. I want to feel that again, and every year, for that matter.

GG: Oh, you'll get there. There is one thing you need to do, Lerita.

LERITA: What is that?

GG: You must ask for what you need, and you have to set boundaries. You cannot do everything and you shouldn't. If people want the big celebration, then everyone needs to pitch in and help with something.

LERITA You are so right, Grace. I hadn't thought about it that way. I have not asked for the help I need. No wonder I've felt so tired and resentful.

GG: If you focus on connection, instead of whether the table is perfectly set or the dinner is a masterpiece, you'll feel the love. The decorations serve as the backdrop for getting people together.

LERITA: Grace, I don't know how to thank you for this conversation. I am so glad that *we* are connected. And Grace?

GG: Yes.

LERITA: Merry Christmas.

GG: Merry Christmas, Lerita.

Reflections

Is the holiday season a happy one for you? Why or why not?

What would you like to happen during the holidays?

How can you experience the holiday spirit every day?

What can you do to nurture the connection among family and friends during the holidays?

Ebony and Ivory
One year after the transplant...

It is January and the first anniversary of the transplant is quickly approaching. I procrastinate for as long as I can before calling Cathy for a couple of reasons. First, I know the holiday season must have been difficult for Jody's family and friends. But I want to break the silence. I need to thank them. I want to let them know how grateful I am to celebrate another holiday season with my family. I work at summoning the courage to pick up the phone. After praying and making several false starts, I call Cathy, and she sounds both delighted and eager to talk to me. We plan a meeting for some time around Valentine's Day at my home.

The other issue lurking beneath my trepidation is race. How is Jody's family going to respond to my being black? I know they are white, but do they realize that I am black? This is Colorado, and I am the first black woman in the University of Colorado Health Science Center's heart transplant program. My correspondence with them reveals nothing about my ethnic or racial background. I worry it might be a real surprise for them. Will an awkwardness surround our initial face-to-face conversations? Oh, why do I have to think about this? Why do I still have to deal with the race issue? It's so draining.

Growing up in Pasadena, California, living and interacting with white people is not new to me. I attended integrated parochial and public schools. I counted among my close friends African Americans, Euro-Americans, Mexican Americans, and Asian Americans. Interpersonal issues around race never emerged until adolescence. In high school, most of my social acquaintances were black, but I will never forget taking classes and hanging out with Greg Yamamoto, Judy Chen, Maria Gonzalez, Karen Johansen, and Isaac Winkler. Later, as I moved out of my hometown, I developed a certain ambivalence about whites. I never knew when I might encounter an open, friendly individual or a racist person who overtly treated me with hatred and contempt.

College presented new challenges in my interracial encounters. In the early '70s, there were mostly upper and upper middle class white and very few black

165

students on the UC Santa Cruz campus. The lack of black students came as no surprise since we were out in the middle of nowhere or, as some remarked, "on the ranch." The physical layout, a college situated in the middle of a forest overlooking the ocean, with non-traditional curricula and professors was not a big draw for black students. Although the whites appeared open and liberal, most of them lacked the multi-cultural learning experiences of my high school classmates. They stared at me in the library and acted surprised—as did many white professors—when I answered a question in class or offered a cogent comment during a discussion.

Graduate school and my first jobs at predominantly white universities were more of the same. Often I was the "only one," a phrase coined by one of my black college classmates to describe our daily existence. I don't think my colleagues here in Colorado have any idea what being a member of a minority group feels like. Likewise, social conversations center on topics they love to discuss; an article appearing in the *New York Times*, the symphony, or the latest expensive restaurant or special wine. They find it odd that I attend church regularly, that I am concerned about my hair, and that I spend a lot of time in the black community of metro Denver. These cultural differences exist, yet I never feel my colleagues express any interest in learning about my culture. It seems they want me to erase my blackness—that ethnic part of me—so I can be more like them. Yet I *am* different and similar at the same time. I love concerts, jazz more than classical, and I read the *New York Times*, sometimes, but not every day. I love great food, although being expensive is not an essential criteria. Unfortunately, due to my medications and allergic reaction to sulfites, I don't drink wine.

The transplant makes me question these unsettled feelings about whites now that a heart from a white woman is beating inside of me and keeping me alive. I don't know where to begin sorting through so much socio-political and emotional baggage. Hopefully, Grace can help me.

LERITA: Grace, I have a question.

GG: Aren't you going to say hello?

LERITA: Oh, hi.

GG: Gee thanks. I mean, you can't even say hello?

166

LERITA: My, aren't you sensitive today?

GG: You are the one who started these conversations, and you seem to think that I should be here—at your disposal—anytime you want to talk.

LERITA: I wanted to ask you a quick question.

GG: I don't merit a "Hello," or "How are you?" before you just start a barrage of questions?

LERITA: What's with you today? Look, I'm sorry that I didn't say hello.

GG: You know lots of people take their hearts for granted. They think we'll pump forever no matter what they say or do. It's a real shock to them when we stop.

LERITA: I bet. Is that what you do, hearts that is, when you get mad, punish us by stopping?

GG: As hearts, we are not vindictive by nature, Lerita. But there is only so much abuse any organ can take. You know livers stop working when they can no longer manage the alcohol abuse and kidneys cannot deal with diabetes and high blood pressure. Worry, anger, hurt and bitterness wear all organs down. For hearts, we can't be happy if it's me, me, me all of the time.

LERITA: I get it. I was wondering if I could simply ask you a question.

GG: Lerita, I know you are sorry that you are so busy that you forgot to say hello and ask me how I am doing. It's ok. I know you can be like that from time-to-time, but I want to remind you to remember the important things; like taking good care of your heart and the people you love.

LERITA: (Mumbling) Where have I heard this before?

GG: What did you say?

LERITA: Oh nothing important. Grace, why am I so tired? I've been struggling for over 12 months now. I go to cardiac rehab. I exercise at home. I still feel exhausted when I come home from work. Will I ever have any energy?

GG: Didn't we talk about this earlier?

LERITA: I guess so. Maybe I need to hear it again.

GG: Haven't we have talked about patience before?

LERITA: Yes.

GG: It's not like you had a simple operation, Lerita. Having a heart transplant requires a major change in lifestyle and attitude. Then there are the physical changes and adjustments to the transplant medications. Considering all that we've been through, I'd say you are doing quite well. The energy will return. What else is bothering you; what did you want to ask?

LERITA: Nothing is *bothering* me, but I'm curious about something, and I think we need to talk.

GG: Then let's talk.

LERITA: You know what it is, don't you?

GG: Yes. You've been mulling it over for some time.

LERITA: Why didn't you bring it up?

GG: Because you're the one having difficulty talking about it. We've had several conversations, and you haven't mentioned it yet. Why are you having such a hard time?

LERITA: Because racial issues are so painful, at least for me. I think about the things that people have done or said over the years because I am black. It's not only a black and white issue. Lots of people all over the world act as if I am contaminated because I am African American. That includes reactions from Latino Americans and Asian Americans and people I encounter in my international travels. Little insults accumulate over the years. I don't understand why, and I am so tired of it.

GG: I think we should start at the beginning.

LERITA: What beginning?

GG: Our beginning. Race was not the issue. Leaving Jody for anybody was. As hearts, we know that under that outer covering everyone is the same. As the essential pump for the body, we have the same purpose for each person, regardless of the race or gender or any other category humans make up. Of course, there is all of the emotional matters we carry, but that varies from person to person and is not necessarily linked to gender and race.

LERITA: Sounds idealistic, Grace. I understand what you are saying but let's get real. I have to live with the outer covering. Tell me this, how does it seem to you pumping inside of a black person instead of a white person? Notice any differences?

GG: Sure there are differences. I had never been to a gospel concert until you took me. I wanted to sing and dance. You and Jody both like jazz and rock and roll. I love them too. She spent more time outdoors and less time reading than you do. I understand your physical stamina plays a role. I know you would be hiking and skiing if you could. There is one major observation I'd like to share.

LERITA: What is that?

GG: Why do people stare at you, uh, at us, so much?

LERITA: There aren't a lot of African Americans living in Boulder, so we're a novelty, especially walking down the street. In psychology, we call it "novel stimuli" and it causes people to stare almost uncontrollably. It perturbed me when I first moved to Colorado. I was very self-conscious. I'm used to it now.

GG: That explanation sounds very intellectual, Lerita, but it's not altogether true or satisfying. The people who stare at us communicate through their hearts, and it's not curiosity that they're conveying.

LERITA: What is it then?

GG: It depends. Some people communicate fear. I cannot understand why anyone would be afraid of us. You are sweet and kind. I know you would never harm anyone.

LERITA: There are lots of people all over the world who are afraid of people of African descent, Grace. The literature would suggest that...

GG: Lerita, wait. The scientific explanations aren't helpful if they don't focus on how it affects you. It troubles you.

LERITA: Like I said, I am used to it, Grace. Take the older white woman at the hairdresser the other day.

GG: The one who recoiled in fear when you sat down under the dryer next to her? You would have thought that you had leprosy or something. She was afraid, repulsed and disgusted; at least that's what her heart communicated even though she flashed a weak smile.

169

LERITA: What did she think I was going to do to her while we were sitting under the dryer at a very nice, integrated salon? It makes me so angry.

GG: That's it, Lerita. You are letting racist behavior upset you. You were having a delightful day, enjoying your time away from the office, and you let her destroy your peace and joy.

LERITA: Grace, you act like I allowed her to make me mad.

GG: You did!

LERITA: How am I supposed to respond to someone who acts like I am tainted or some ogre! It's humiliating and I was livid.

GG: Don't take it in.

LERITA: Don't take what in?

GG: Her misguided perceptions, her feelings. Don't let them touch *you or me*; don't allow them to seep inside. It's a situation that requires you to set boundaries around your heart. If she isn't aware that you are a human spirit just like her, then let that error stay with her. The hate and repulsion will damage her heart and her body, but it does not have to injure yours unless you choose to send that hate back. The anger only increases your blood pressure. You should feel sorry for people like her. Can you imagine what life is like inside of her mind, in her inner world? Her poor little heart is nearly paralyzed by all of that fear and anxiety. What kind of inner peace and joy can she experience if she can't sit down next to another person in a beauty salon? I'm sure she hears lots of voices.

LERITA: Voices? You think she has a mental problem?

GG: I guess you could say anyone with that much fear has mental problems. I'm certain the hyperactive chattering, those fear thoughts that are bellowing through her mind all of the time, make her tense and anxious. I'm sure glad I'm not her heart. Her heart space is too cluttered to sing and dance. The stench must be unbearable.

LERITA: Fear stinks too?

GG: Yes. Fear coupled with contempt is the worst. It will stop a heart.

LERITA: What does fear smell like?

GG: I am trying to find words to explain an odor like that. Probably a decaying body is the best description I can render. Fear and contempt are sure pathways to death. I would need to wear a mask if I had to pump her heart. Lerita, there is something you need to understand.

LERITA: What is that?

GG: There are only spiritual beings in the world. However, most people identify solely with their physical bodies and what those bodies represent.

LERITA: Please say more. I am not quite certain I understand what you mean.

GG: Everyone is a spirit, but some spirits appear to be black, white, Asian, or Latin, for example. The classifications constructed differ, from country to country, by region, or by city or village. But remember, they are spirits first. Unfortunately, people are unaware they are spirits and *think* of themselves as their bodily label—"I am a white man," "I am a black woman," "I am a Latino professor," "I am an Asian gay man," "I am an Indian writer."

LERITA: This is so fascinating. I have never thought about people primarily as spirits. I actually teach about ethnic and racial identity in my class. Where did you get the primacy of the spirit part?

GG: It emerges as natural wisdom of the heart. However, you have to open your mind and heart to hear and accept such notions. Clearing away the debris in your heart allows your spiritual heart to override your other constructed selves.

LERITA: I am speechless. What a different way to think about race. I mean race or gender, ethnic background—easily discernible physical attributes that represent what sociologist Erving Goffman calls "master status." He pointed out that people initially respond to a person's master status and all of the stereotypes associated with it. Help me to understand this further. You say that there are people who *appear* to be white, black, etc…and other people who *think* of themselves as black, white, etc.? What's the difference?

GG: Again, people who do not realize that they are spirits think of themselves and others based on their "master status," as you call it. People who *know* they are spirits *appear* to be a member of a category. Yet they *know* their social category is not who they truly are.

LERITA: How does one gain that knowledge? Do some people just wake up one day and *know*?

GG: Some do. Usually, the knowledge emerges from some kind of spiritual awakening. It may come from a crisis like yours or some experience of joy or through prayer and meditation. I guess the most important element is a willingness to be open to seeing people and the world through a different lens.

LERITA: That kind of perception would involve a major paradigm shift and then some!

GG: Unfortunately, in the case of the woman under the hairdryer, both of you were living out the typical race mindset. Your reaction wasn't only to her; it was an accumulation of feelings. It brought up other racial slurs or insults you've experienced. You must find a way to let go of the feelings rooted in old hurt and pain and find another way to be in the world.

LERITA: You've mentioned this before. Letting go takes time, Grace. I can see that this new way of perceiving might speed things up for me.

GG: Maintaining love despite the expression of another's hateful feelings is the most healing thing you can do for both of you. Sending hate back to her means there are now two people who are sick in their hearts. Think of those who haven't experienced a spiritual awakening as being deeply asleep.

LERITA: I can remember Heavy Harvey mentioning something about being in a deep sleep, but I don't think I can initiate a spiritual awakening for myself or anyone else, Grace.

GG: Don't you see why you have to, Lerita? If you detest everyone who sends you hate or fear every day, you'll never be happy. Look at the agitation that this one incident caused you. Where is the peace and joy that you yearn for? True spiritual maturity equips you to maintain love for a suffering spirit whose heart is burdened with hate and fear. In the spiritual realm, they are like little children—possibly wounded somewhere along the way and now using you as a scapegoat.

LERITA: The ones that annoy me most are the people walking around Boulder and acting like I am some interloper who shouldn't be out enjoying all that the city has to offer. Many people don't speak or make eye contact when I say hello.

It's hard. I grew up in a culture and community where you were taught to speak, to acknowledge people when you see them on the street.

GG: Sometimes there are cultural, regional and generational differences for those responses, Lerita. In some cultures, people are taught not to make eye contact. Some individuals are so disconnected from themselves that they have difficulty bonding with anyone. Sometimes fears about racial and cultural differences are piled on top of that. Again, their behavior may not have anything to do with you or your skin color.

LERITA: It just seems like they're picking on me.

GG: Lerita, you are not a victim. They are not picking on you in particular. Ignore them. Pray for them. Pray that they will soon find some relief for the gnawing fear or hate they feel inside. Pray that they, too, will uncover their spiritual heart. If you are going to get angry, at least put the energy to good use.

LERITA: How do I do that?

GG: Wasn't it Duke Ellington who said, "I merely took the energy it takes to pout and wrote some blues." Do something constructive with your outrage, your anger. Write. Teach someone to read. Make a new dish. Use your talents, your intellect, and your love of sewing; cultivate this gift of spiritual wisdom to help someone else.

LERITA: Gosh, Heavy told me the exact same thing. Grace, you know about Duke Ellington?

GG: It bears repeating. And yes, Lerita, I know about Duke Ellington. Jody's Dad played big band music in the house all of the time. She liked most music and the extraordinary music the likes of Duke Ellington is enjoyed by people all over the world. Similar to Jody, there are many people who are not spewing hate.

LERITA: Did Jody know she was a spirit?

GG: She was slowly waking up to the idea. I believe she sensed that she was connected to all people in some way.

LERITA: I know that not all people are racists or sexist. Remember that guy we passed on campus, the one with the knapsack on his back?

GG: Yes. He made eye contact, his smile was genuine and he said hello.

LERITA: He definitely wasn't a student. Usually, they are so self-absorbed and have absolutely no manners.

GG: See, there you go getting upset again, Lerita. It's the same problem of disconnection and lack of knowledge about one's self, especially one's authentic self. I will repeat this one more time—not everything is about you, Lerita. Please don't turn other people's issues into a statement about your character or who you are. It's one of the worst forms of egocentrism because you keep attacking yourself.

LERITA: That's true. About three-quarters of the seniors I teach don't have a clue about who they are when they begin my course on self-concept. Do you think there is a relationship between knowledge of yourself and racism or speaking to and being kind to strangers?

GG: Again, some of it is cultural. But you can always sense what's in someone's heart. Don't you think you have become kinder and more open to others as you've grown to know yourself? Don't you treat yourself with more gentleness?

LERITA: I'll have to sit with these ideas and questions awhile. I have another question for you.

GG: What is it?

LERITA: How did Jody deal with black people?

GG: Jody didn't know any black people other than her customers who came into Casual Corner. She grew up in Wisconsin, in an area where she didn't have much contact with blacks, except those she saw on television, until she moved to Colorado. Although Jody had regular black customers, she didn't have any African American families in her neighborhood. She treated them like she would want to be treated.

LERITA: Television was the only way that she knew about African Americans? That's pretty scary.

GG: She learned about other groups of people mostly from newspapers and magazines, although sometimes she read a few books by African-American writers. It's hard to remember now, somebody named Walker?

LERITA: Alice Walker, *The Color Purple*.

GG: That sounds right.

LERITA: Was Jody afraid of African Americans?

GG: She was cautious about anyone she didn't know well. She watched lots of sitcoms with African Americans, and there was the evening news. I think her perceptions were affected by what she saw. But her heart was open to everyone. I know if you sat down next to her at a hair salon, she would have smiled and welcomed you. Like I said, she believed that all people are united in some way. She also learned to trust her gut. She remained approachable unless someone said or behaved in a manner to cause her to act otherwise. Some people are good. Some people you should avoid because their intentions and thoughts are evil, and they are not in their right minds.

LERITA: I finally learned that lesson myself. I used to smile at everybody. I was socialized to be nice even if the person might be an ax-murderer. But some people are best left alone. You don't mind being in the body of a black person?

GG: Why would I? My functions are the same. I pump blood, hold your feelings, encourage you to love, and share the wisdom of the spirit within your heart. Sure, there are cultural differences, different activities sometimes. Because Jody was around people who looked like her, she didn't have to put up with the staring and strange reactions. Don't you think these experiences have made you...?

LERITA: Stronger? I hear that stereotype all of the time. Dealing with racism builds character. I wish we could find some better ways to cultivate inner strength. I am happy, though, to have my life, my family and my culture. I wouldn't want to be in any other race or ethnic group, despite the idiocy I am subjected to sometimes. I also understand that I am not just a black woman. I am so much more. My race and gender define my experiences to a certain degree, but they do not begin to represent all of who I am.

GG: That's beautiful, Lerita.

LERITA: Hey, I'm glad we talked.

GG: So am I. That's been on your chest for a while.

LERITA: Sounds like a heart pun to me, Grace.

GG: It's only a figure of speech, Lerita.

LERITA: (Laughing) OK. I'll talk with you later.

GG: I look forward to it.

Reflections

How much and what kind of contact do you have with people who appear physically or culturally different from you?

Were you exposed to different racial or ethnic groups growing up? If so, what did you learn about the similarities and differences?

Have you ever lived in a place or been in a situation where you were a minority? How did you feel if people stared at you?

How do you think viewing others through the lens of your heart might affect how you feel about them?

Have you ever perceived yourself as a spirit? Have you ever experienced others as spirits?

Love and Marriage?
About eighteen months after the transplant...

I sit staring at an album of childhood pictures and reminisce about my life as the "almost" bride. One photo shows me smiling in my first Halloween costume, a bridal gown with veil. The next picture is of me wearing a similar frilly white dress on a hot summer day when my brother married Davey (the little boy down the street) and me in front of a large maple tree. Ah, here's the photo of me as a flower girl in Cousin John's wedding, dressed in a white lace dress with a ribbon of rosebuds flowing down the back. I remember how strange it felt to be four years old and have people stare, clap and smile as I pranced down the long aisle in that magnificent church. In another photo, I am at 7 years old, third from the end on the second row in my Holy Communion class, feeling like a bride again with a white dress and veil. Then there is my senior prom where I wore my custom-made debutante dress—also white like all the mock bridal gowns from childhood.

I realize that I've been set up from an early age to seek and find a husband. I edge closer to the altar when I served as a bridesmaid in several weddings. With great anticipation, I peruse bridal magazines while standing in line at the supermarket, yet somehow marriage eludes me. Now, at 43, as an African-American woman with a heart transplant, I have three strikes against me. I guess if I count the Ph.D., that's four strikes. Getting struck by lightning is four times more likely than a marriage proposal. Yet I hold a speck of hope in my new heart that I'll marry someday.

As an unmarried woman, I receive tons of unsolicited advice on my love life. "You should attend another church." "You should date white men or Asian men or Latino men." "You should move to another city, another state, another region of the country, another country." "Your standards are too high." Before she died, my grandmother told me two things: "When it comes to a man, never settle; life is too short to not get what you want;" and "When you meet the right man, you'll *know* it." I am not quite sure what she meant by *"knowing,"* but I understand it hasn't happened yet, well not until last weekend.

I travel to Washington, D.C. for an academic conference and decide to contact one of my old colleagues, Myron Brown, a professor at American

University. I last saw Myron 12 years ago, although we communicated infrequently via email or phone. I call when I arrive, and Myron suggests that I join him and some friends for dinner on Friday night. Myron's plan allows us to catch up and I can meet some new people as well.

Unfortunately for my beautifully coiffed hair, the skies open up, pouring buckets of rain as I step into the entrance of FICA'S Restaurant, a short taxi ride from my hotel. I sit down to a table set for four and avert eye contact with any lone men in the room. Long distance relationships are not my cup of tea.

Minutes later, in walks Myron with a gorgeous Gambian woman named Evelyn and another guy he introduces as Warren. Warren is Myron's brother, and despite all the years I've known Myron, I had never met his brother. Immediately I feel some weird connection with Warren. I wonder if we had encountered each other someplace before. I ask Warren a few questions to pinpoint the occasion to no avail.

I notice, too, that Warren and I like similar menu items and we begin sharing food like an old married couple. I turn to Myron to remark about this strange coincidence when Evelyn looks at me and asks, "Have you and Warren met before?" Apparently, two connections are in motion—between Myron and Evelyn and Warren and me. Then Warren pipes in that we met on a beach many years ago, and I tripped him. I turn to smile at Warren over the crazy tale he conjures up, and I hear a voice inside my head say, "*This is your husband but not right now.*" I think, "Where did *that* comment come from?" Warren is cute, but he didn't look like my type, whatever that is. A big, teddy bear kind of guy with pretty brown eyes and slightly graying, balding hair, Warren appears to be the quintessential nice guy. Undoubtedly, this isn't my future husband—or is it? Then, as our eyes meet again, and like my grandmother predicted, I have that *feeling*. It is similar to the one I had prior to my heart transplant when I heard, "Do not fear. You will survive the transplant." A deep, unworldly sensation resonating in the bones and all of the cells of my body chime in, "This *is* 'Mr. Right.'"

LERITA: Grace, Grace. I've got some great news.

GG: I was wondering when you were going to contact me. You think about him all of the time, and these thoughts make you very happy.

LERITA: You already know?

GG: It's obvious to everyone that you have that look of infatuation, that glow.

LERITA: Yes, it's the first time in a very long time I've felt this way. When I think of him, I feel a sense of rightness, almost a oneness, like we are supposed to be together.

GG: Your fairy tale has a happy ending.

LERITA: It does?

GG: Yes. You're going to marry him.

LERITA: What? What did you say?

GG: I said you're going to marry him.

LERITA: I was thinking that would be nice, and I heard this voice saying that when I started talking with him. It was so weird. ...But I've thought "this is the one" in the past, and I've always been so disappointed when it didn't happen. How do you know I'm going to marry Warren?

GG: Remember Lerita, your spiritual heart lies beneath your surface emotions. We know things before they reach your conscious awareness. It's like intuition.

LERITA: Is that why I felt like I had a premonition that I would marry him on the first night I met him? It was so strange. When he first walked in the room, he seemed familiar, like we had met before. Then we started talking and sharing food. You know I don't believe in soul mates, but I certainly felt connected to him immediately.

GG: Precisely.

LERITA: He doesn't look like my type. I mean I'm not sure if I would have picked him out of a line-up of potential "Mr. Rights."

GG: Didn't you ask God to send you a mate?

LERITA: Yes, I've been praying about that for a while, especially since the transplant.

GG: Unlike lust, decisions of the Spirit aren't based on physical attributes, Lerita. You know some of the best gifts in life aren't always wrapped in gorgeous paper or come in small burgundy boxes. Besides, don't you think he's cute?

LERITA: He's definitely cute, but a different kind of handsome than what I'm used to. He has a more rugged, outdoorsman's type of attractiveness.

GG: If you've suffered many disappointments in the past, this might be an excellent time for you to take it slow. I suspect you've been enticed by

179

handsome men before. I don't want you to jump in too fast and have everything collapse. If you do that, I will have to carry the funky feelings when it's over.

LERITA: I wasn't expecting to hear that from you, Grace, but I agree. Given my dating history, I'm definitely in need of some new practices. I'm tired of getting my hopes up and having them dashed into a heap of disillusionment.

GG: After that heavy load of disappointment that Heavy hauled away, I appreciate that you are willing to try a different approach to your love life. Tell me more about Warren.

LERITA: What more is there to say? Since I think about him all of the time, you know about him already, Grace.

GG: Yes, but I want to hear all of the juicy details from you. Oh, this is so exciting! Jody would be so happy. She always wanted to get married and have a family.

LERITA: I think meeting him was divine intervention. It occurred 40 days and 40 nights after I heard some inner voice say, "You've had a transplant. It is time for you to get married."

GG: I bet that serious forgiveness work around all of your old hurts and disappointments helped a great deal.

LERITA: Yeah, that was hard. I didn't know I was carrying such deep contempt for men until Heavy pointed it out.

GG: No wonder you weren't having much luck in love, Lerita. With that kind of resentment, you didn't have much room for anything else in your heart.

LERITA: Let's get back to Warren. He is smart, kind and extremely considerate. We both cherish great food, art and art museums, nature and being together. From the very beginning, he felt right. It was like we had been together forever. Being with him is as comfortable as putting on my house slippers. There's only one problem.

GG: What's that?

LERITA: He lives in Florida.

GG: Why is that a problem?

LERITA: I live in Colorado! That makes him G. U.

GG: G. U.? I've never heard of that. He's not married is he, Lerita? I am sure I didn't pick that up.

LERITA: No, no. I mean he was married, but he's recently divorced. No, it means "geographically undesirable."

GG: (Laughing) Right.

LERITA: We're talking about a serious phone bill and the cost of plane tickets to Florida. It could get expensive.

GG: There's always email.

LERITA: That's not quite as intimate as I'd like, if you know what I mean.

GG: That's the beauty of it, Lerita. From what you tell me, you're always in a rush to fall in love. The distance will give you time to get to know each other. Then you can have some long-lasting intimacy instead of that, "passion in a flash" some people think is intimacy but isn't.

LERITA: You've got a point, Grace. It's been so long since I've had anyone in my life. I wish I could be with him every minute of every day and …

GG: Uh, Lerita, wait until you're married. You may be singing a different tune.

LERITA: I cannot imagine not wanting to be with him all of the time, Grace.

GG: Would you like me to fast forward you five years to the middle of your third year of marriage?

LERITA: You can do that?

GG: For you, Lerita. Just for you.

LERITA: I don't understand how hearts can play life forward as if it is on some kind of recording device.

GG: It's a little heart secret. I want you to listen to this:

(Lerita on the phone): Oh, Barbara, I've got to find Warren a tennis buddy. Yeah, he needs to be out with the guys. He wants to be around me all of the time. And I am so tired of cleaning the stuff in the sink that he leaves. What? No, he doesn't always wash the dishes, and there's some clutter. I don't understand. His house didn't look like this when I visited. It was always so clean, and everything was put away. Between the two of us, there are clothes and personal items everywhere…Oh, yes he has a business trip next week. I need some time to myself, just a few days would help, so I can breathe and spend some time with my girlfriends. I know, I know when we were dating, I couldn't wait to see him…Yes, those weekends were so intense, and we were so far away from each other. I only saw him every six weeks or so. I guess I didn't think being married would be like this…Yes; it is hard to live with someone else, especially a husband (laughing). I guess that's what I get for marrying so late…Oh yeah? The third year is when the disillusionment sets in? Really? Yeah. I'll get through it…Ok. Barbara. I'll talk with you later…Yes, it's been almost 30 years for you and Melvin…Wow, that's truly inspiring…Yes, we must talk again soon…Ok. Bye…

LERITA: Grace, that's unbelievable. Are you sure that's me talking?

GG: Yes, Lerita. Relationships evolve. Emotions ebb and flow. It's not always going to be so passionate and intense.

LERITA: I am going to get bored and disinterested after a while? I didn't wait this long to be unhappily married.

GG: No, no, Lerita. You will have to develop the glue that keeps relationships together no matter what, during boredom or through good or hard times.

LERITA: How do I do that?

GG: Couples like you and Warren have to learn what it is that makes each other's heart sing and practice it frequently.

LERITA: Huh? I am supposed to make Warren's heart sing? Aren't I doing that already by being in love with him?

GG: That's infatuation. There may be special things that he likes, such as a home-cooked meal after a business trip, or rubbing his back in bed at night, or maybe he likes a special kind of flower, like peonies or roses.

LERITA: How would I know that? I am not a mind reader.

GG: It's something you *learn* as you are *getting to know* Warren. Beyond the physical attraction is a whole inner world to explore. That's real intimacy, when each of you shares your deepest thoughts, desires, and dreams. It is so important for you to know what brings joy and sorrow to his heart. He needs to learn the same about you.

LERITA: I'm not sure if I know what makes my own heart sing.

GG: Then you better start thinking about it and make a list. I've only been with you for a little while, and I know several things.

LERITA: Like what?

GG: You love tulips and Dutch irises. You also like a meal cooked especially for you as well as a bath in candlelight. We know that anything related to tea or sewing, especially unusual teapots and gorgeous fabric, bring you joy.

LERITA: That's true, and a massage wouldn't hurt.

GG: Doing things that make each other's heart sing is the essence of a happy relationship. That joy is the glue that holds you two together during the tough times and when Warren naturally does things that are destined to get on your nerves. It goes with living with someone other than you. Marriage will help you both grow in so many ways. Practicing doses of "just let it go" kind of forgiveness will also create the happy home you both desire.

LERITA: This conversation is very enlightening, Grace. Thanks so much.

GG: Oh, it's my pleasure, Lerita. I look forward to you finally being in a relationship that will make us both want to sing and dance.

LERITA: I am happy for us too, Grace. I'll talk with you later.

GG: Alright.

Reflections

What are you hoping for in your heart?

Are there things in your heart, like disappointment or resentment, that you need to let go of to make room for a new relationship or transform a current one?

Do you know what makes your heart sing? Do you know what makes the hearts sing of people in your life—a parent, spouse, child or friend?

Letting My Heart Be My Guide
About 21 months after the transplant...

Like the first year of marriage, nothing and no one could have prepared Grace and me for our life together. Clearly, there were challenges that Grace and I encountered as we tried to knit together a partnership. Neither of us liked the changing assortment of pills or medical procedures like biopsies and heart catheterizations. We both learned to cultivate patience with each other and with our communication patterns. We also understood that we weren't a perfect match, but our connection worked.

The greatest gift of a life-threatening event like a transplant was an increase in clarity. I realized I didn't like my work environment. I wasted most of my time and energy attempting to gain full acceptance from my colleagues and the profession. Somehow I always felt they pitied me. "Poor Lerita, with all of her medical issues." "She is never going to be a 'star' in the field." Evidently, I needed a new vocation in another location.

A painful insight seeped into my mind during the many days and nights lying in hospital beds and at home. For most of my life, I hadn't followed my heart; my ego led the way. As Heavy Harvey and I discovered in our early conversations, I wanted to be that star, to have fame and fortune. When was I ever going to learn to listen and follow my Spirit-inspired heart rather than the ego-driven chatter in my head? As I reflected on my life journey, I could see that somewhere I took a detour. Now I needed to return to the path of the heart, the seat of peace and joy. Unfortunately, it took a heart transplant and all of the accompanying suffering to uncover this insight.

Now I know that *listening* to my heart is key. My heart is filled with eternal wisdom and guidance. Yet, I often confuse thoughts generated by my own driven nature with intuition or my heart's desire. I see the fear wrapped up in my desperate need for love and yearnings for recognition. I used to believe that the promise land was out there somewhere if I could only reach it. I am learning that life is not about being a successful psychology professor. In fact, my salvation lies not outside of me at all. It is inside, and it begins with my heart.

My hearts gently nudged me in another direction, away from the stressful and crazy expeditions of the ego. Heavy Harvey reminded me that real stars don't *try* to shine, they just do. When was I going to stop being so competitive? When was I going to get off the track or put down the racket and live a happier life as he advised? How many times have I heard a Voice trying to warn me about a potential boyfriend or a project or an event? Like Heavy Harvey said, our hearts send us red flags all of the time.

Grace stresses the importance of letting go of negative emotions regularly so that my heart can be full of the goodwill that her name symbolizes. No wonder poor Heavy Harvey couldn't pump anymore. There was nothing worse for hearts than to live with funky emotions and a heavy load of baggage. Grace also reminds me about faith, trust, patience, surrender, love, connection, and relaxation. When I cultivate the courage to follow my heart, the joy is simply and wonderfully present.

Twenty-one months had passed since the transplant that joined us together in this arranged marriage of sorts. My life was finally feeling "normal." I liked checking in on occasion, but Grace had a different idea. Here is what transpired in our final heart-to-heart conversation.

GG: Lerita.

LERITA: (no answer)

GG: Lerita.

LERITA: (no answer)

GG: La-reet-taa!

LERITA: Grace, is that you?

GG: Yes, it is.

LERITA: Sorry. I've been so busy trying to keep up with the new semester. I cannot believe all of the work that keeps piling up.

GG: You sound excited.

LERITA: I know. Usually, I'm depressed at this point. It's not that I don't like teaching; it's so intense. In contrast to the summer when activities slow down, each semester I am bombarded with meetings, manuscripts, conferences,

185

students, and letters of recommendation. The list is endless. Among my colleagues, we have a joke that the title Ph.D. really means that the work is **P**iled **Hi**gher and **D**eeper. Sometimes I feel I don't have a moment to breathe.

GG: Is it different this year, now that you've had a new heart for over 21 months?

LERITA: Yes, in some ways my life is transformed. Having the transplant helped me to see all of the artificial divisions I'd placed in my life. Work is a demanding obligation and leisure is fun. Relationships are challenging, yet I've discovered new friends and realized how much people love me. I decided that work could be fun if I stopped putting so much pressure on myself. I've been working steadily all year, but not frantically.

GG: Sounds like a great change.

LERITA: It's strange, Grace. I am at the time in my recovery when if I had chosen not to have the transplant, I would be dead. And if I were dead, I wouldn't be worrying about the semester or many issues that I used to think were so important. I have such a different perspective on my life now.

GG: I'm glad to hear that. You sound peaceful.

LERITA: I'm getting there, slowly but surely. I've been so busy that I forgot that we haven't talked in a while. Do you have something that you want to discuss?

GG: Actually I do. We've come a long way together in our recovery. Don't you think it's time we get back to acting normal?

LERITA: You think there's something abnormal happening?

GG: Yes, Lerita. I mean these talking sessions. It's not the normal way that hearts communicate.

LERITA: You don't like our conversations? I thought you enjoyed them.

GG: Oh, they are very nice. But they are, uh, not natural.

LERITA: Unnatural?

GG: Lerita, most hearts don't talk, they communicate through *feelings*. Because of the unusual circumstances of the heart transplant, talking was crucial to our adjustment period and recovery. Don't you think we know each other well now? I mean, I would still like to communicate with you, but in an ordinary way.

LERITA: I understand how you feel, Grace. I've learned so much from these conversations that I've shared with you and Heavy Harvey. I guess I knew some things, but I needed to hear them presented in a different way. Are you sure you want to quit talking?

GG: For now. Your health seems fairly stable. And you aren't thinking about killing yourself.

LERITA: I am far beyond those thoughts, Grace. Don't worry. I realize that my feelings travel with me wherever I go. When I started these conversations, I didn't understand how much was weighing down my heart. Poor Heavy. If I had known earlier, we could have stayed together.

GG: Maybe. Now you understand why you need to monitor your thoughts and especially your feelings and moods. You must also pay attention to how you respond to things, to people. You are quite reactive.

LERITA: Yes, I guess I could work on not letting people and their behavior upset me.

GG: Lerita, I think we are both lucky to have each other. I appreciate your efforts to quiet your mind, your attempts to listen to the messages I send and to keep your heart space clear so I have lots of room to sing and dance. I like your love for the earth's natural beauty, the mountains, how you stop to take in the sun on glistening snow in the winter and to savor a late day thunderstorm in the summer. You take time to watch a golden sunset, to water the flowers in your garden, to sew and read, to engage in those activities that make us both want to sing and dance. I don't think that I could have found a better body, a better match.

LERITA: Thanks, Grace. I am also grateful, despite my earlier whining and complaining, for you, my new, well not-so-new heart. My life feels lighter. Some of my contentment I know is due to the emotional load that Heavy Harvey took with him and to his wise counsel. I'll never forget what he told me about the big four, *listen, trust (the Guidance), patience, and surrender*, principles that I needed to master to succeed with the transplant and my life. It's like I had a chance to start over without being born again as a baby. And I am fortunate to have you. I remember when you told me about your name—that it symbolized unmerited favor and a reprieve. With the heart transplant, I was granted more time to heal and become whole. Grace, you are so sympathetic, helpful, and wise. Your counsel, especially during these 21 months of a roller coaster recovery, is like nothing that I've ever received—anywhere and from anyone. So, is this goodbye?

GG: Oh no. We will talk from time-to-time. In fact, when you and Warren get married, and you will, you may need to check in during the first couple of years. They will be a bit challenging for you, especially since you will come to marriage as an older bride who is set in her ways.

LERITA: You are certain Warren and I are going to get married? We just met. And yes, I suppose I will need some guidance as we get adjusted. But what about the relationship…how am I going to develop the relationship since he lives so far away?

GG: Trust me, Lerita. Everything will work out, but it will require you to be extremely patient and to listen faithfully to me, your heart. If you continue to pause and listen from within, to follow my urgings, you'll be able to hear me even better. It's like everything else—being a star athlete, a talented musician or writer, or gifted artist—*practice* is essential. Will you promise to practice listening daily?

LERITA: Yes, I promise.

GG: It is extremely important for you to pause and be still regularly. Feeling the urgings of your heart or hearing the little voice is not easy, especially when you constantly listen to the radio or watch television. Then there is that relentless chatter in your mind that you engage in much of the time. You're pretty good, but most people do not pay attention to their lives, to their bodies, and especially to their hearts. They ignore their feelings, but emotions are the best signaling device around. If something doesn't feel right, stop and be still. If you are angry or sad, ask yourself why and what must you do to address the issue and whatever is underneath it. If you feel some deep psychic pain that you try to escape by keeping busy, eating or watching television, then it's time for you to pull out the teddy bear and tissues. When I am not singing and dancing, something is awry.

LERITA: I will listen, Grace. I'm going to miss these conversations. But, if I know that I can call you, to talk like this anytime and you will answer, I know I will survive.

GG: More than survive, Lerita. Thrive. We'll thrive together.

LERITA: I can't seem to get that word, "good-bye" out of my mouth. It's too hard.

GG: Don't say it. Know that I am always here. You can feel me beating, can't you?

LERITA: Oh yes, all of the time.

GG: Good. Can you feel that?

LERITA: That's a heart-hug. Heavy gave me one before he left. Can I say it, Grace? Can I call it a heart-warming moment?

GG: (Sighing) If you must, Lerita.

LERITA: I love you, Grace.

GG: I love you, Lerita.

Reflections

Have you ever felt like your life took a detour? Have you sought guidance about how to return to the path of your heart?

For what are you grateful?

What do you need to do in order to thrive?

Are you now ready to have a conversation with your heart?

Today, I will…

Epilogue

As I sit at my desk writing this epilogue some 24 years after the transplant, I marvel at the transformations I've made along the journey. I am no longer angry about my medical issues and the subsequent "disruptions" to my life. In fact, I am thankful for this life crisis that propelled me toward the path of the heart. How different the scenery looks now that I've accepted rather than resisted a journey that focuses on living from my heart and not my ego-driven self.

I am grateful I elected to have the transplant as I muse over the occasions and experiences I would have missed had I chosen to die instead. I cherish the wonderful memories of my parents' 50th wedding anniversary. Celebrating with extended family, including former members of my parents' wedding party, all healthy and full of joy, was an event I was delighted to witness in person. I cannot imagine life without my loving husband, Warren. Meeting him, falling in love, and getting married (finally!) were such jubilant occasions made particularly poignant because I had survived the heart transplant. I know these events would have remained improbable had I not experienced the personal transformations that came with making a change in heart. Yes, marriage continues to be demanding for both of us, partly because I am a transplant recipient.

My transplant experiences did not cease after 21 months of conversations with Grace. I continued to be challenged by a major bout with organ rejection in 2003, which resulted in a 27-day hospital visit. The battle to treat my rejection with a multitude of strong drugs sometimes made me feel like I was going to die, and led to a prognosis of renal failure. That tested my faith and trust in my hearts and God. I spent a year on dialysis and then received a kidney transplant nearly 14 years ago, an ordeal that tested the depths of my marriage and my personal relationship with Spirit. My medical difficulties persisted with additional heart surgery to replace a valve on my transplanted heart along with the addition of a pacemaker in 2006.

Being loved by Warren, chest scars and all, created a bond beyond words. I find it hard to believe that I've been blessed with such a kind, sweet spirit of a man, who was clearly designed to be my life partner. We continue to teach and learn so much from each other.

Opening up my heart, looking inside and deciding to address the sinkhole full of emotions I discovered remains one of my most difficult yet best achievements. Slowly releasing all of the disappointment, anger, shame, and insecurity provided such a gift. I love the peace and joy that stem from carrying a lighter heart, a heart that has room to sing and dance and overflows with love. However, I am not immune to the human experiences that elicit irritations, annoyances, disappointments, and sadness. After my conversations with Grace, I am now more aware of when my heart feels bogged down, and my peace and joy are obstructed. My daily spiritual practice of listening prayer/meditation and journaling centers on eliminating the things that block my peace and joy

Perhaps the greatest gift I received, more than an extension of my bodily life, was the spiritual awakening that accompanied the transplant experience. I had a long-standing interest in spirituality, but because of the unpredictable nature of the transplant experience, I cultivated a stronger and deeper relationship with God. I began to listen to Spirit guiding me in the quiet and to trust its Guidance. Daily, I work to develop more patience and practice surrendering.

My determined and tenacious personality gave me the strength and courage to meet the transplants head-on, but I needed some deeper understanding about why I was experiencing so much physical suffering and close brushes with death. I sought to learn more about how people all over the world understand and express their spiritual selves. I learned that at the core of most faith traditions is the admonition to forgive, to express compassion and love for one another. I trained to become a spiritual director/companion and now take great joy in sitting with people, listening to their sacred stories and encouraging them on their spiritual journeys. I lead workshops and retreats on listening prayer/meditation, give talks on my favorite mystic, Howard Thurman, and teach everyone I can about being still and listening from within.

Recently, I have begun to lead Heart Talk workshops to assist individuals and groups by creating conversations with their own hearts. I continue to write about how to maintain a peaceful and joyful heart on my website, peaceforhearts.com. I want all people to be able to access the Spirit which resides in their hearts, to discover the heart that lies beyond the one that beats relentlessly, and carries all of our emotional burdens. I attempt to point the way to the part of our hearts that seeks to guide and lead us through the frenetic world we perceive. My desire henceforth is to keep Grace a happy heart and to share the wisdom of both of my hearts with all who are willing to listen.

Appendix
Instructions for Having Your Own Heart Conversations

Tools

Spiral notebook or yellow pad or several blank pages.

Favorite pen or smooth writing instrument.

1. Find a quiet, comfortable location where you will not be disturbed or distracted by anyone for at least 30 minutes.
2. Start the conversation by saying hello to your heart.
3. If your heart doesn't answer initially, try coaxing it with a gentle salutation (e.g., "Hi Heart. I know we have never talked to each other, but I would really like to speak with you today. Do you have a minute?"). It may sound kooky, but it works.
4. Once your heart answers, you might begin with a topic you would like some guidance about. Ask a direct question. Begin handwriting the dialogues.
5. Often the conversation will go in an unexpected direction. Just let it happen.
6. Write for at least 30 minutes, longer if it seems right to continue.
7. When you are finished, please tell your heart "thank you."
8. Your heart may or may not reveal its name in the first conversation, but if you ask later, it will tell you.

Group Exercise

1. This exercise can be conducted with a group that has established ground rules around confidentiality and emotional and psychological safety.

2. One person should be assigned the role of group facilitator and timekeeper. Each member of the group should initiate a conversation

with his or her heart, following the guidelines above. The group facilitator should alert the group members when ten and five minutes remain.

3. Group members may or may not choose to share what emerged from their conversations with their hearts. It is best to allow each person time to share without comments or questions, unless the person sharing, requests it.

$17.95

ISBN 978-0-578-73011-0

51795>

9 780578 730110